# in Justice

## A STORY OF TRUTH
## ABBEY M. BLUE

WESTBOW
PRESS®
A DIVISION OF THOMAS NELSON
& ZONDERVAN

WestBow Press books may be ordered through booksellers or by contacting:

WestBow Press
A Division of Thomas Nelson & Zondervan
1663 Liberty Drive
Bloomington, IN 47403
www.westbowpress.com
1 (866) 928-1240

ISBN: 978-1-9736-0290-3 (sc)
ISBN: 978-1-9736-0291-0 (e)

Library of Congress Control Number: 2017914482

Print information available on the last page.

WestBow Press rev. date: 11/29/2017

## A note from the author

Abbey Blue represents the unheard voices of trauma.

Writing this book has been a profound process for me.

I believe written words have the ability to squash the silent fears that linger in us as a result of the traumas of life.

I am no expert and I do not consider myself a teacher, nor do I desire to lead anyone to do things how I have done them.

We walk our own paths.

My hope is that after reading this book, the reader is left with a greater understanding that our voices do matter and I hope the courage it takes to speak out becomes something you receive for your own journey.

No matter where you are from or what you have dealt with, I hope you receive the circle of forgiveness that I know is all around you ... so you can give it to others.

# Acknowledgements

a Snapshot of Gratitude:

To my parents and grandparents: I wish you could have read this book. I suppose you are behind the bookcase already knowing. Thank you for leaving me the gift of your words – leading me to mine.

To my children: I will always be in the bleachers cheering you on. Thank you for being my main audience for this story. Always be you and know that I love you muchly.

To my uncles, aunts and cousins: Thank you from the bottom of my heart for being my first friends, for understanding and knowing the little girl in me. And for accepting me 'as is'. Thank you for laughing, crying and digging in the attic with me. Let's watch those home movies with popcorn and apples soon.

To all my friends (and I have many) who have waited patiently to read this story: Thank you for walking with me and knowing my name. I love my Nest of Sparrows, Band of Women (I cherish the song we sing), Chicks of God, Country Bumpkins and Tidal Wave BFF's. You have no idea how much empowerment you give me. Thank you for believing me.

To my ignited girls: Thank you for dotting my I's and crossing my T's … and for carrying me to the finish line. There are no words and yet, we still yearn to express them. I hope we sit around the table for our next books.

To Mama W: Thank you for hugging me and never letting go. I love you so very much for adopting me into your heart. I love our zig-zagging, rabbit hole, day long talks, topped off with laughing our butts off. Always my mother, always my friend; surely He has these hearts.

To my sister: You are my always and forever. Thank you for always being the strongest big sis this gal could have. I can't imagine my life without you and I'm grateful that no matter what, I never have to. Thank you for taking the doors and finding the writing on the wall. I love you so much for being that person in my life.

To my husband: I don't know where we are goane', but you will always be with me.

To my GPS, Jesus: Thank you for loving me so wholly.

# Contents

## Prologue

The sound of my feet echoed against the drab walls as I traipsed down the darkened hallway. No other sound could be heard; even my thoughts were silenced. I could make out the long row of doors due to the dim light coming from the end of the long hallway, but as I walked toward the light source, it seemed to get farther and farther away.

There was nothing in this mysterious hallway—no chairs, no windows, no pictures hung on the walls—and if there was a roof, it couldn't be seen with the human eye. There was a long row of doors on either side of the hallway. The only way out, it appeared, would be through one of these doors.

With so many to choose from, which one should I open? I chose the first one that I came to, on the right-hand side of the hallway. It was just a simple gray door on the right. As I slowly opened the door, I squinted as the light flooded past me into the dark hallway, followed by the musty smell of old books and chalk dust.

The room was full of elementary-aged students, most of whom were hunched over their desks and appeared to be writing. Perhaps it was a classroom assignment or a maybe a test. One girl in the front had been reading to the whole class. I could not hear what she was saying, but apparently she was done, because everyone began to clap and cheer. She was high-fived by a boy as she returned down the row of desks to her seat. The boy giggled as the girl passed him, blushing as his buddy next to him punched his arm.

Two girls in the corner passed notes and giggled together. One boy wrote on his hand with a marker. Another boy smeared Elmer's glue over the palm of his hand. He blew on it, waiting for it to dry so he could peel it off.

Everyone waited as the teacher walked to the front of the class, and then several hands were raised as high as they could go and the room was filled with the excitement of going next. "Me, pick me!" several kids yelled out. A few others said nothing but stared at the teacher with laser eyes, as if they could telepathically convince her they were her best choice.

The anticipation was thick, and it seemed the whole class wanted to go next, except for the girl sitting in the middle of the last row, next to the window. She stared out and didn't seem to notice what was going on around her. She had a glazed look on her face. I barely recognized her, but it was *me*.

"Okay, everyone calm down. Everyone will get a turn," the teacher stated. Coming out of her daze, the girl turned toward the teacher and fumbled nervously with her papers. I could see that she was anxious, as her foot was tapping vigorously under her desk, but she slowly raised her hand. She turned to stare blankly out the window again. Her telepathic message seemed to be, "I'm ready, but please don't pick me. I'm too scared."

"Well, Abbey, come on up and share your poem with the class. Now remember, boys and girls, be quiet and pay attention to the reader. Our written words are important, and we need to respect each others' time in front of the class."

The girl took her paper and made her way to the front of the class. She stood there staring at her classmates, and her paper trembled in her hand. I could see it from where I stood at the door.

She stood there silently, stared down at her paper, and then looked up at her classmates. She opened her mouth twice, only to be met with hollow silence.

There was a bit of rustling from the back of the room as a girl passed a note to her friend. The two snickered together at Abbey's obvious stage fright. As the boy with dried glue started peeling off his artistic masterpiece, the teacher got up, ready to encourage the poor girl who stood so nervously in front of the class.

Abbey's eyes grew bigger, and tears began to form. She stared at her shaking paper and realized what was happening. Warm liquid streamed down her leg. Because she was wearing a dress, the wetness was not obvious right away, but it was only a matter of time before they would know.

She knew there was no way out of this horrible situation, so she froze. She couldn't cry. She couldn't scream. She couldn't run. She just stood there listening as the puddle formed on the floor between her legs. With the stench of urine overcoming her senses, she watched as the rest of the class caught on to her nightmare. Their laughter and ridiculing words became muffled and distant as she slipped away into the zone, escaping the horrific reality of her little girl life.

I was no longer alone in the dark hallway. The little girl and I stood together, peering in the opened door to the past. She looked up at me as if asking me what she should do.

Her eyes held such sadness and grief. I needed my eyes to be reassuring and confident. She needed me to have answers.

The memory of that moment from my childhood flooded my heart, hitting me like a tidal wave. Except now, all these years later, I knew something I hadn't known then; while I knew the damaging effect of my classmates' ridicule, I also now knew that some of them had been kind.

With smiling eyes, I brushed her hair back behind her ear and pulled her close to me. "Let's just look for a moment longer, okay?" She nodded in agreement and leaned in to me as we watched the scene inside the classroom continue.

"Oh dear, Abbey. Well, I ... um ... Let's just get you to the nurse and get you fixed up, okay?" The teacher stammered on and clumsily took the girl's paper, placing it on her desk. In the teacher's nervousness, the girl's unspoken words got pushed under the stack of the teacher's other paperwork, never to be seen again.

"Leroy, walk Abbey up to the nurse's office." The boy, done peeling the glue from his hand, jumped up and walked toward the door—but without the girl. Abbey stood still, frozen and unable to move, knowing there would be a trail of wet footsteps the moment she took that first step.

"Go on, Abbey. Get yourself to the nurse and get yourself changed," the teacher said, a little too harshly, causing her to shrink further into her nightmare.

Leroy walked over and put his arms around the girl. He whispered, "It's okay, Abbey. I've done it too. I had to walk all the way home in my soaked britches one time." Abbey looked at him blankly, but all she could really hear or see were the kids who were doubled over in laughter as the girl was led out of the room with the unmistakable trail of disaster that were her wet footprints following her.

As we stood in the hallway, the moment froze as I

looked down at the little girl and she up at me. "Did you see that? That boy, Leroy, wanted to reassure you. Did you hear what he said? It happened to him once too. He understands and you are not alone. You're going to be okay. It's going to be all right."

The tears flowed like a river, and she rubbed her eyes with balled-up fists as I held her and we let the tears of embarrassment flow.

After a while, she peeked back in the door to see the moment frozen in time—that moment when her heart was so broken that she had missed the compassion of a friend. That moment when her heart became hard because *they*, the others in life, left a bigger impact than the compassion of a true friend.

Leroy's hands were on her shoulders while her head hung low as they walked to the nurse's office. Her face was red, her expression dazed. The shock was obvious.

"Yeah, I see him now. I didn't notice him before. I couldn't even hear him. All's I could hear were the other kids laughing at me. Now I can feel his hands on my shoulders." She looked up at me again, and our eyes locked. The red-eyed little girl's face softened, as did mine. Looking back through the door, we could see the scene before us start up again.

They were now in the school nurse's office, where Ms. Margaret looked up from her desk with a big smile. "Hi, honey doll. What's bothering you today?" Ms. Margaret was so matter of fact. She was different from the other adults that Abbey knew.

Ms. Margaret had helped when Abbey accidentally jumped off a big rock and onto a rusty nail in a board lying on the ground in the playground last year. She had taken charge of the situation and reassured Abbey that everything would be okay. She had called Abbey's mom, staying with her until she was picked up. Her presence alone kept Abbey calm that day.

Abbey stood before Ms. Margaret with her head down. "I peed my pants." The tears flowed as she relived the nightmare from ten minutes earlier.

Bending down and looking through her bottom drawer, the nurse said, "Let me get you taken care, of honey doll. I just happen to have a new package of panties here that are just your size. I might even have some socks too. Yes, look, I do! We will get you all cleaned up and like new, okay?"

Ms. Margaret stood and walked over to the girl, putting her arm around her shoulder and leading her toward the private bathroom in the nurse office. "You can go now, Leroy." He skipped off.

"They all laughed at me, Ms. Margaret, and I want to go home. Can I please just go home? Can you call my mom?"

"We are having none of that, missy. We'll get you all cleaned up ... Let's take a look at your dress." Ms. Margaret pulled at the bottom of Abbey's dress. "You didn't even get your dress wet! As for those kids, sticks and stones, lovey, sticks and stones. You know their words can't hurt you." She handed me the panties and socks and pointed to the bathroom. "Get on in there and change so we can get you back to class."

"B-but, Ms. Margaret ...," Abbey stammered, trying to figure out how to tell Ms. Margaret that she was wrong about sticks and stones and words and stuff, that their words had cut her in half and that she simply could not face them again.

All these years later and from where I now stood, in the hallway, I knew she stammered because she wasn't able to tell Ms. Margaret that she felt abandoned by her parents since the divorce. She didn't know the words worthy of the rejection she felt as her mother replaced her with a new man and her father moved across the country. She wasn't able to articulate the pain she felt or identify the neglect. She just knew it hurt.

Her friends, it seemed, were all she felt that she had left. It *did* matter what her friends thought of her because everyone else in her life had let her down.

I could now see that others were defining her because she didn't know how to do that on her own just yet. They had a powerful impact on her identity. They had the power to build her up or tear her down. Looking back, it was easy to see that the odds were against her at this point.

She only knew the deep hurt and confusion. She didn't know it wasn't all up to her. She didn't know what to do *at all*. So she did what any child under that kind of stress would do. She created a safe, protected space for herself—a place no one else could enter. A division was created that day. There was Abbey … and there was everyone else. *They* were created. *They* were given power over her, to harm her, to define her. Her only perception of protecting herself was to disconnect from them all, at times even including herself. Abbey disappeared as she walked into the bathroom and shut the door. The click of the lock echoed in my ears.

I looked down, but the little girl was gone. I stood alone. I desperately wanted to go back and save her from becoming trapped in the locked room. The door I had opened was now shut. The scene had disappeared, and try as I might, the door would not open again.

I had lost her, and I didn't know what to do. I could no longer see the end of the hallway, which seemed to go on forever. I tried a door across the way, hoping it would open and I would find Abbey or, if nothing else, find my own way out. My heart sank as I discovered the door was locked.

I ran the long corridor, panicked, trying each door, finding them all locked. Pushing against the knobs didn't help. Kicking didn't help. Neither did screaming. Standing there, out of breath from my frenzied attempts for freedom, I realized the only thing before me was a long path of locked doors to which I didn't have a key.

The funny thing is that I didn't even think to knock.

# Chapter 1

## *Time for Flight*

San Diego, 2008

Surprisingly, the hinges didn't break as I slammed the trunk as hard as I could. Having just emptied the taxicab of my baggage, I felt as if I were going to collapse from the heavy load.

"Thanks, buddy!" I sarcastically yelled to the taxi driver as he sat behind the wheel, viewing my frustration from his rearview mirror. I glared and silently swore at him because my bags were way too heavy for me to carry alone. Somehow I'd managed to get them out of the trunk without breaking my arm.

At that moment, a car whizzed by me, and I felt the sudden whoosh of the near hit. "Go ahead and do it!" I yelled to the driver as I looked up toward the sky, talking to the real person in charge. The truth was that in that moment, I'd rather be hit by the speeding car than take the flight I was about to take.

The anger quickly turned to fear and engulfed me as I threw all my bags and myself to the ground. "Aaargh! I don't want to do this!" I sat there for a moment while travelers gawked at me. Some laughed, some smirked, some shook their heads, and one guy even said "Crazy lady!" as he led his family away from where I sat.

Embarrassed, I got up and gathered my bags—again somehow managing to do the impossible by carrying all the weight of my baggage alone.

The walk through the airport terminal was long and arduous. There were moments when I envisioned what it would look like to drop the bags and just start running—sort of like Forrest Gump, except I had a reason for running. I could run for miles and miles and still not escape the fear of what I needed to face: the past.

The thoughts went through my head like a speeding train without brakes. *This all happened so long ago! Why on earth would you be going back to drudge it all up now ... Let it go ... You will never be able to let this go ... Once a victim, always a victim ... You've already ruined your kids' lives ... Your life is a joke ... No man really wants you ... You aren't whole; you are useless.*

My heart was beating ridiculously fast, and the familiar pain in my stomach urged me to find a bathroom—and fast! I did not want to throw up in the airport entrance. Luckily, I found myself in front of a bathroom and ran into a private stall before I hurled.

Afterward, as I washed my hands, I avoided the mirror, as always.

*Noooo!* I thought to myself. *This madness is going to stop.* The thoughts that had imprisoned me motivated me to get my bags checked in, acquire my boarding pass, and continue through to airport security.

My thoughts raced again. *I can't live this way anymore. I've been stuck behind a locked door that I haven't been able to get through, as hard as I try. I don't feel right. I don't feel whole, and I know it has to change.* I practically screamed, "If this is what it is going to take to get my life back, then let's do this!"

"Hi, ma'am. How are ya? You'll have to remove your shoes, and if you have a belt on"—his eyes scanned my body, stopping at my waist—"then remove that too."

There wasn't even a smile left in me at this point. The usual mask of "I'm fine" had been torn off in the parking lot. The smirk I give him was far from a smile.

Finally making it to my assigned gate, I flopped into a chair and took a deep breath. I'd made it, and for that, hallelujah.

"Mommy!" the kid next to me screeched, while the young woman sitting next to her ignored the child and adjusted her reading glasses.

*Are you kidding me? Do you not hear your child, lady?*

"*Mommy!*" The child was now pulling on her mother's leg and trying to rouse her attention away from the book the mother was reading.

*It must be a real page-turner.* I wanted to grab the child and tell her to settle down—and then I wanted to take the book and knock the mom upside the head. *When will the noise stop already!*

Closing my eyes, I began to again envision myself running. This time I saw myself running out of the airport and back home to my children, who were only thirty minutes from the San Diego airport, yet they were miles and miles away, emotionally speaking. As quickly as I began to imagine walking in the door of a home surrounded by a white-picketed fence, with kids smiling and running toward their mommy as she entered, reality struck.

The home I would have been running back to would be an empty apartment filled only with darkness and depression. The home I wanted no longer existed; it was broken, and I was the one who broke it. The kids, well, they still lived surrounded by the perfect white-picketed fence with their dad—but without me.

My inward anger and unresolved pain had turned outward, and my family had finally had enough of my emotional outbursts mixed with bouts of isolation and depression. My unrealistic need to be loved and understood was filled with alcohol and another man who was not my husband; I had destroyed our family, and they'd all left me … when I left them. I walked away expecting them to stay put and wait for me to get whole and to come back home. But kids need their parents to be present. I knew the only way to come home to them was to go back to my original home—back to where the assurance of home was taken away from me.

I was returning home to Little Mountain, Kentucky, in search of the home that had been taken away so many years ago when I left to escape the shame.

My silent hope for strength quickly became a prayer for peace. *God, please give me the peace I need to get on this plane.*

To drown out the noise from not just the screaming kid but also all the airport's commotion that pierced my aching head, I grabbed my Bible. Needing comfort, peace, and courage to face the demons of my past, I sat for a minute with my hands on it. I silently prayed for God to give me something substantial to lean on. Just having the book on my lap and the familiarity of the words gave me the faith I needed. *I can do this.*

"Well, that's refreshing to see." I looked up to see a man in khaki pants and a white dress shirt, my space invaded yet again by a stranger.

"Excuse me?" *Who is this guy?*

He sat down next to me. Pointing to my lap, he said, "Your reading preference."

"Oh. Thank you." Wanting him out of my personal space, I turned away from him, wondering what he really wanted.

As if reading my mind, he moved in front of me and pointed to his wedding ring. "I'm a happily married man. I hope I didn't come across too forward with you."

"Umm ... okay."

"And ... I'm a pastor. I just thought it was nice to see a young person with the Bible in public."

Something in me softened. *Maybe I'm just too paranoid. I mean, he is a pastor, for goodness' sake!*

"I'm sorry. I'm just very anxious about flying, and, well, I am a little grumpy ... Not at my best today."

"Nervous ninny for flyin', eh?"

"Yes. I'm a big scaredy-cat. I've only flown a handful of times, and each time I about have a heart attack. Getting here was a joke, and I was late—and, well, I'm a C-boarding passenger today." I showed him my boarding pass with the number C-60 printed on it. "I will be the last to board." He grimaced as I said the words.

The loudspeaker interrupted us. "All A passengers for flight 2747 from San Diego to Nashville, Tennessee. Please line up now."

"That's me." He gathered his belongings and stood up.

"Lucky you!" I said, my voice laced with sarcasm.

He turned back toward me. "Hey, would you like me to save you a seat next to me in the front?" He pointed to his wedding ring again. "I promise that it's a happy marriage and I mean no harm," he said with a smile.

"I suppose. Umm ..." Thoughts of a major anxiety attack

hitting me in the back row of the plane helped me quickly decide to take him up on his offer. "Yes, that would be very nice of you. Thank you."

*I mean, seriously, he can't harm me on a public plane.*

# Chapter 2

# *The Man on the Plane*

Fumbling with my overstuffed bag, I boarded the plane and quickly felt the doom of being on a full flight. The claustrophobia kicked into full gear, and I scanned the seats for my pastor friend—he was about 7 rows back, looking out the window, appearing to be deep in tranquil thought. With the storm brewing inside me, I was definitely not calm. I felt encapsulated by vulnerability and fear. The seat to his right was empty, but a rather large man occupied the aisle seat.

*Yikes, what have I gotten myself into?* Looking around the plane I saw that there were no other seats available, I was, after all, the last one on the plane. I made my way toward him and stood staring at the big guy in the aisle seat.

My presence seemed to bring the pastor out of his calm trance. "Ah, there you are," he said, gesturing for me to take the middle seat.

The big guy on the aisle seat sighed deeply as he got up to let me in. Plopping into the seat with much relief, I said, "Wow, thank you so much." As I stuffed my belongings under the seat in front of me, I secretly hoped that they wouldn't fit and I'd get booted from the plane because of luggage restrictions. Once the bags were snuggly in place and my foot was protectively on my bag, I exhaled.

I leaned my head back, and all I could hear was the beating of my racing heart. *Is my heartbeat so loud that they can hear it? Can I just disappear right now?*

Deciding I needed my own space, at least until we were airborne, I closed my eyes and talked to my heart. *It's going to be okay. The sounds are normal, and the small space is not going to kill you. Claustrophobia will not kill you—it's just uncomfortable, and this too, shall pass.* Deep breaths in, deep breaths out, like childbirth. I needed a focal point, but if I opened my eyes, I'd be opening myself up to conversation, and I didn't want that right now, so with eyes closed and mind focused, I "swung it out."

The freedom of swinging has always been my escape. As a little girl, it was my go-to when I was stressed or scared. Even in my imagination, the sound of the swing's chain above me and the swishing of the wind blowing through my hair always seemed to drown out my worries. With legs pumping and feet reaching the clouds, I soared.

The jumping in my stomach told me that the plane had just leveled out and that we had survived the takeoff, so I opened my eyes and took in my surroundings.

Big Guy next to me was reading his book, and the pastor was lost in thought again. Not wanting to disturb him, I focused on reading my *SkyMall* magazine and figured I'd kill some time thumbing through that. Maybe this would be a quiet five hours. I welcomed the relief.

"Feeling okay?"

"Yes. Thank you, Pastor, for saving me a seat. I appreciate it so much."

"It was no problem. Are you staying in Nashville?" *So much for a quiet five hours.*

"Well, kind of. I'm a professional photographer, and I'm going there to photograph a wedding with a colleague, but then after the wedding, I'm going to drive home to see my family for the week. This is my first of two trips as I'm hired for a second wedding in just three weeks from now! It's a small town in Kentucky a few hours away. What about you? Family in Nashville?"

"No, I'm going for a pastoral convention. What part of Kentucky is your family from?"

"Oh, it's a very small town that you probably won't know of ... It's called Little Mountain, Kentucky."

"Nice. You're right ... Never heard of it." He chuckled.

"Yeah, I've never met anyone yet who knew where it was. It's a small town. It'll be interesting to go back and see how it's changed. I left when I was thirteen years old."

"How long has it been since you've visited?"

"About twenty-five years."

"Wow! This is a big homecoming, then, isn't it?"

"I suppose so. It's a long story."

"We've got almost five hours. Can you tell it in that amount of time?" He chuckled again.

"Well, umm ... I don't know. I've never told it to a stranger before."

"I'd like to listen if you'd like to tell it."

And so, my small town story began.

"In Little Mountain, Kentucky, friends reside not just right down the street but across the way, across town, and on every street in between. Small towns breed big hearts and strong friendships. Small-town friends meet in kindergarten and grow old together. Never really leaving.

"Most small-town folks stay in their small towns. They may physically move on to another place, another building, but they are always home in Little Mountain.

"Small-town friends discover how to like, love, fight with, separate from, and dance with and around all of life's rites of passages. They pass on to first grade together and play on the playground together. They do Brownies, Girl Scouts, majorettes, track, and skip school on snow days together.

"They do the awkwardness of middle school together. They do braces, puberty, and not 'fitting in' together.

"They do the excitement of high school together. They do basketball games, spring breaks, and first loves together. They do proms and walk for graduation together.

"They have not just lived life together, but they are also connected for life. But for me, life's connections were interrupted and Little Mountain became the mountain in my life that needed to be moved.

"At thirteen, I got lost and never really found my way back home. Shame, guilt, and embarrassment bordered my hometown, keeping me out. I have spent my life believing that I don't belong in the place that I know as 'home.'

"I said it has been twenty-five years since I've been home. But the truth is, I have been back a few times to visit my immediate family; however, on those visits, I hid because I felt like an intruder in my hometown. I walked around believing the lie."

The pastor held up his hand. "Wait, you got lost? What does that mean? What happened?"

*Can I really do this?* I was acutely aware of the people surrounding us; I glanced over at Big Guy, who now appeared to be napping. The people in front and back of us were lost in their own conversations.

*Yes, I can. And with my chin up.*

"I was raped. I mean, not raped ... Yes ... raped ... Honestly, I don't know what to call it because they are not

10

legally rapists. I got drunk for the first time with some kids I didn't know, a few girls and their boyfriends, and I was raped by the boys," I said, looking at my lap. As I lifted my eyes to the pastor's, I didn't see the expected condemnation, just tears welling up in his eyes.

"I am so sorry, Abigail." He wiped away his tears.

"No need—it's not your fault!" It was such a funny feeling to hear a man apologize for a stranger's wrongdoing. His apology didn't penetrate. How could it? He didn't do this horrible thing to me.

"So then what happened? Where did you go?" he asked.

"Well, after the court case, I ended up in California with my father, a long-distance truck driver. My mother stayed home in Little Mountain."

"So they were convicted and *you* left town?"

"No, there was no conviction. They were acquitted. They got a 'not guilty,' while I took the 'guilty' verdict upon myself. And technically, only one of the boys, the adult, he was the only one with charges filed against him. I don't really know why. I was so young and the adults made the decisions."

"But you were thirteen. How old were they?"

"Sixteen, sixteen, seventeen, and nineteen years old. Technically, only three of them did it to me. The fourth one got me home the next morning." As I said it, I realized that I still had a hard time with the word *rape*.

"How on earth did they get acquitted?" he asked, his eyes wide with wonder.

"That's what I'm going home to find out. I am on a search for justice. I don't want legal justice ... It's been way too long to expect that. I just want to know for myself how it could have happened. It's personal justice that I'm seeking. There is so much that I don't remember and so much that I

11

have compartmentalized in my mind. It was all too much for a teenage girl who was just hitting puberty, so I pushed it all down and away, at least until I had kids. When I had my own children, I was forced to deal with my issues and my healing journey began. It's been a rough road, emotionally speaking. I've made a million mistakes, and I've had some healing …a lot of counseling … and my children are grown now and it's my turn. Something is missing from my healing. My burning question is *why?* Why wasn't I believed? Honestly, if all that happens is that I am able to look at least one of those boys in the eye, without even saying a word to him, I'll be satisfied. I want to look the real perpetrators in the eye and stop seeing the one I blame in the mirror."

"Wow! Where are you starting? What's your plan?"

"Here's the cool part of my story. Last Easter I was home, alone and completely depressed, and I was watching *Dateline*. A woman was telling her story. It was similar to mine in that the crime had happened two decades earlier, and at that time, she had no legal justice. She pushed it aside and went on to have a successful life. All these years later, her perp, who was going through a recovery program, wanted to make amends with her and reached out to her asking for forgiveness. She forgave him, but she also prosecuted him because there was no statute of limitations. She got both legal and personal justice. Her story somehow awoke my desire to be exonerated, even if it is just a personal kind of freedom.

"Deciding to finally do something about it, I got in touch with her on Facebook. She encouraged me to go forward in my search for personal justice. With so little recollection of this time in my life, one of my biggest desires was to remember what I had said in court. I told her I'd probably never receive the thing I really wanted, which was to know how a jury could let them off the hook but that I'd take what I could get.

"I ordered the court transcripts and then prayed for God to open doors. And He sure did! A few weeks later, the paperwork I received was not the transcripts but all the administrative paperwork from the court. Included were the subpoenas and petitions, as well as a handwritten list of about thirty-five names. Twelve were underlined, and one was starred, with the word *foreman* next to it. I had a list of the jury members in my hand. I didn't know how I was going to reach out to these people, but a week later I received a phone call from my photographer friend who lives in Nashville. She asked me if I would assist her with two weddings she had just booked! I had not just one, but two paid vacations a couple hours away from my hometown!"

The pastor's mouth was open in shock. "You have got to be kiddin' me!"

"Nope. I don't know what I'm doing with it just yet, but I have it right here," I replied, pointing to my bag underneath the seat.

"Abigail, this is unbelievable."

And there it was, my worst fear verbalized: that no one would believe me.

"I know," was all I could muster.

"So when this all happened to you, was your father there with you?" The pastor leaned back, crossing his arms.

"No, he was in California already and had been for several years. He wasn't allowed to be there. I was always told that he'd been kicked out of town and told not to return. You know that small-town mentality depicted in the movies? Well, I always pictured that to be real for my dad, being shunned by the small town we lived in ... Well, it isn't surprising to imagine that ... Anyway, I do remember that he wrote letters to me. I just can't remember what he said to me. I know he was supportive, but really, all I remember about the letters is that in one, he sent a drawing of a little girl and on it were the words 'God don't make no junk.'"

Continuing, I said, "The words in the letters apparently weren't that important to me then, though I'd love to hear them now, but that picture has stuck with me over the years. I'm hoping that this experience is going to bring the words to life. I need my identity to change from feeling like junk to believing I am a treasure, like the Bible describes me to be."

"Where is your dad now … and how does he feel about you doing all this by yourself? How does your mother feel about you coming home with this jury list? Does she know?"

"My mom doesn't really have an opinion on it—at least, I haven't asked her if she has one—and my dad is dead. But I'm not doing it alone." Leaning forward, I grabbed my Bible and held it up. "Abba, my Father in heaven, is doing this with me."

"Yes, God is with you for sure," he said, nodding his head in agreement.

"No … I mean, yes, God is absolutely with me … I know He has orchestrated all this … but my dad and I are connected through this Bible. He gave it to me several years ago, and I never opened it, not until after he died. And when I did … *wow*! We reconnected. I totally get that it isn't my Dad, Terry, talking, that it's my Abba, God. I get it … But the words on these pages … they were just words on pages. God was not familiar to me. And until I could hear a familiar voice saying them to me, I couldn't know the … I mean, it's not an audible voice, but in my head, I can picture my dad saying these things to me. Teaching me. These words came alive for me when my dad died."

Just then, Big Guy shifted, reminding me that there were other people around us. He got up to go the bathroom.

"I'd better hit the bathroom too before the aisles are filled up," the pastor said, leaving me alone in the aisle but acutely aware of the *they* on the plane, surrounding me.

# Chapter 3

# *Where the Ribbon Fell*

With both men gone, I secretly wished I had the whole row to myself for the duration of the flight. I imagined what it would be like to curl up in a ball and just sleep. Knowing that wasn't going to happen, I looked down, admiring the soft pink cover that reminded me that I was his little girl.

As I opened it, Dad's handwriting caught my eye, which caused my heart to ache. Instantly I was taken back to the day several years ago when I found this book while unpacking a box.

I envisioned my father's rough hands writing such gentle words. Dad's hands were rugged and strong yet beautiful and so capable of this gentleness. Those hands were skilled in doing just about anything around the house, including making the world's best peanut butter and jelly/hot chocolate combo. The same hands capable of producing discipline also gently wiped away the tears that escaped my eyes, caused by the pain of punishment.

As an artist, his hands created beautiful sketches. He would draw while my adoring eyes simply took him in, mesmerized, his eyes squinted, focusing as he transferred the image from his mind onto paper. Dad always wanted to teach me how to draw, but I just liked to watch. His process of shading was hypnotic for us both; all we needed was a pencil and a piece of paper to be enthralled for hours.

As an Italian, hand gestures were a language to Dad. His arms would flail sporadically as he raised his voice so that there would be no doubt you could hear him, and he ended most statements with fingers bunched together and in your face as he said, "Capisce?" He needed to know you fully understood him. The fist bump against his chest was my favorite because it was filled with much emotion.

As a child, I marveled at my father's strength and gentleness toward me. I was the apple of his eye, and his hands were my favorite, holding my hand and my heart, offering comfort, safety, and help as I grew into my own person.

It couldn't have been easy for my father to reunite with his traumatized teen daughter. I was not easy to live with when I came to California. I wanted his love, but I made him fight for it. I resisted every one of his attempts to help me. I rejected him, yet he never stopped trying. As a teen, the offer for counseling was always available; I just never took him up on it. Nevertheless, we managed to stay close, as close as I would allow anyway.

And then the really big division happened. It wasn't just the trauma of the rape. It was the rape partnering with his alcoholism. I needed safety and healing, but the pain overtook us both in our own ways. We eventually grew apart but never completely away from each other. At some point, I grew out of my rebellion, settling down with a family and wanting more, but by then, Dad's hands seemed to always have a drink in them, keeping us distant.

Now it was too late. He was dead. It happened so suddenly—he was just gone. His best friend found his body lying on the kitchen floor. No more chances. No more time to mend our relationship.

A tear dropped on the thin Bible page, smudging the treasured handwriting:

*To my daughter, for when you need strength*

*Merry Christmas 1996*

*Love, Dad*

"Ha! I should be giving this Bible to you!" I said to him the day he gifted it to me. I was half joking, but he needed this book much more than I did. *Didn't he?* It seemed our roles were reversed, him in the role of an adolescent and my playing the parent. *I* was the one who had been in counseling. *I* was the one who could hold down a marriage and a job. *I* was the one who could be there for my children. *I* was the one who attended church every Sunday. I mean, *I* was the healthy one. *Right?*

Besides, regarding the Bible, as far as I was concerned, I believed that while God inspired the Bible, I also believed that man wrote it, man read it, and man interpreted it. I liked owning one, but deep down I believed that man ruined it. The popular Sunday school stories stood out in my mind, and I certainly read this cherished book, but it was just an old book that didn't give me answers. I didn't believe there was any correlation between the ancient Old Testament and my everyday life.

As I sat there looking at the inscribed words from my dad, I, the one who had judged him so harshly, now marveled at the power of these simple handwritten words comforting my empty soul.

My wandering thoughts took me back to one of the many days I had to pick him up from the bar. The day he peed his pants in my car was one of the most painful times between us. The joke he tried to crack in the car that night didn't cover the embarrassment and humiliation in his eyes. My heart still breaks remembering that.

My thoughts returned to the book, and I opened it to where the pink ribbon lay. The ribbon was in this same place the day I found it. I tend to keep it there to remind me. The ribbon fell in the book of Ephesians 3:8, which says, "Although I am less than the least of all God's people, this grace was given me: to preach to the Gentiles the unsearchable riches of Christ, and to make plain to everyone the administration of this mystery." Near the end of his life, Dad was less than the least to me. It seemed that his failures were my only memories of him. The regrets of all that was taken from me, from us, overruled the love and respect that was buried deep within me.

All the times of picking him up at the bar because he couldn't drive, the times he didn't show up to our family events, or the times when he *did* show up and I told him to leave because he reeked of alcohol and stale jokes from the night before—those times I remember clearly. The years of abandonment and letdowns left me thinking very little of my father when he died. Looking back, I had no idea the impact the words on these two pages would have on my life over the next year.

Where the ribbon fell in this book directed me to the beautiful pages of Ephesians 3:8 through 5:7. The truth of walking as a believer in Christ came alive.

I found my father's heart.

It took about a year truly to take in so much truth, but as I read and asked God to move in my life, I began learning what it was like to be a Christian. It wasn't about the rules and the regulations. It wasn't about judgment and self-preservation. It was about seeing his power strengthening my inner being. It was about prayer that established me in love—love so wide, so deep, so long, and so high that it surpasses human knowledge. It was about living a life of humility and gentleness, patiently bearing with one another in love, and keeping unity. It was an understanding that we all have our own gifts and that we need each other to be built up in these gifts. We need the knowledge of the Son of God to become mature. It was about a love that grows in us, and it was about speaking truth in love. It was about working hard and sharing with those in need. It was about changing my words from unwholesome to words that would build another up. It was about trading bitterness and rage for compassion and forgiveness. It was about being imitators of Christ.

It was also about boundaries and not partnering with those who didn't honor God and who were full of empty words.

These lessons started with the first sentence on the top left page and ended with the last sentence on the right-hand side of the page where the ribbon fell in the beautiful book on the day I finally opened it. My connection to hearing from God, my heavenly Father, was the very words that my earthly dad, Terry, gifted to me, the Bible. I suppose, in the end, Dad came through with an incredible gift that would last eternally.

I was gifted some incredible experiences as I committed to reading this book of revelation. With my head back and eyes closed, I allowed the memories to flow, remembering how I had learned about my own father from a mere barfly.

The bar was busy, but there he was, a permanent fixture on his stool. I knew I'd find him here.

"Sal, hi …" I pushed a twenty-dollar bill into his hand. "Take this to use for a taxi and show up. Dad would want you at his memorial. Please … don't *not* come. It would have meant a lot to him to know you made it."

"Well, hiii, girllll," he slurred. "I ain't gonna miss your daddy's funeral. He is … was … is … my best friend." His tears dripped onto the bar.

"I know, Sal. I know." I watched as he crumpled up the bill and pushed it deep into his pocket. I pointed toward his pocket, questioning my judgment in giving a raging alcoholic my hard-earned money. "Please don't drink that away. Get in a cab in three hours, okay? I wrote the address on a Post-it note, and it's with the money in your pocket."

"You're a good one, Abbey."

The feelings evoked just by his saying that name were intense. Not too many called me Abbey—only a select few—and Sal wasn't one of them. But Dad was, and he must've referred to me as Abbey when talking with his friend. Anger rose in me, and had I not been running around crazy with last minute preparations for the funeral, I would have politely and sternly told him that my name is Abigail, *not* Abbey. But I wanted him to be there. I didn't want to upset him, so I let it go.

Walking away, all I could do was hope he'd make it. *Why was I trying so hard to get him there?*

Three hours later, in the windy park, I was standing with my children and my ex-husband, and of course Sal wasn't there. Several people had shown up, and we all stood under the gazebo. All his daughters were there—Anne and me as well as his two ex-stepdaughters whom Dad considered to be like his daughters—as well as all our children and several close friends of Anne's and mine.

The box with his cremated body was in the middle of

our circle. I remember thinking that it made no sense to me that his 6'4" body fit in that tiny box. Stanley, Dad's boss, was the main speaker. I had met Stanley at a company Christmas party a few years earlier, when I was Dad's date. During a conversation, Stanley had made reference to being a believer of the Lord. When Dad died, I didn't know who else to ask to lead his memorial. Stanley kindly accepted when I called to ask him. At that time, he told me it was his honor because he and Dad had been meeting for two years to pray and read the Bible together. He told me that Dad has accepted the Lord as his personal Savior. I remember being in such shock, but I had an immediate joy in knowing that Dad believed in God.

The wind died down just as Stanley stepped forward to begin speaking. The leaves on the trees were no longer moving, and the air became still and peaceful. It was then that Sal noisily got out of the cab and joined the celebration. We all watched as he stumbled to his place beside Dad's other friends from his apartment complex.

Memorials are bittersweet. They bring out the best in people, and emotions are highly charged. Dad's was no different. My emotions, along with my words, were stuck in my throat. I found it very difficult to speak, and I cried through partially spoken words when it was my turn to share. Luckily, Anne came through and was able to speak for both of us. After the family spoke, we had an open microphone for others to share their memories.

Sal went first, and anger arose within me. I could smell the alcohol on him as he walked past me and toward the front of the crowd. I wanted to boot him out. After all, I was good at booting out alcoholics.

A couple of years ago at Christmas, I booted Dad from our house. I told him to leave our home because I couldn't stand the memories my children were accumulating of their grandfather. I wanted the memories to end for me as well. I wanted perfect memories for the kids, so I controlled the situation and told him he needed to go home. I didn't care how he was getting home or what he'd be doing for Christmas dinner; I just knew I couldn't take care of him anymore.

Sal stumbled to the front and began his eulogy. "Terry was my best friend. My life is better because of him. I have a life today because of his friendship. I met him two Christmases ago. He reached out a hand to me and pulled me up. Literally. I was sitting in an alley, and I was homeless and drunk. My daughter hated me, and I wanted to die. But there was Terry. That day, he nudged me and said, 'Hey, bud, come on upstairs and eat. No one should be alone on Christmas Day.' He reached his hand out to me and pulled me up. He helped me get a job. Yes, in a bar, and no, I haven't quit drinkin'. But I pay my bills and my daughter is in my life. And I want to live. I will miss my best friend. Thank you."

One by one, Dad's friends all stood up and told how Dad had affected their lives. Whether it was his smile and daily 'good morning' as he stood on the balcony smoking his morning cigarette or the way he opened his house for the community barbecue, they each spoke of the things that affected them. They saw a good friend, and I saw a failure of a man who drank and smoked his life away.

Because he was not their father, they were able to see all layers of Terry, a troubled alcoholic but a man with an open and kind heart. I felt the shift that day—the shift of seeing the person of Terry as opposed to the loser alcoholic.

After the memorial, Anne, our stepsisters, and I went to the beach and spread his ashes at the edge of the ocean.

We laughed and cried as we let him go. I was ecstatic over what Stanley had said earlier at the memorial: Dad was in heaven. When we were done, we sat on a bench overlooking the water, claiming that particular spot as his.

About a week after the memorial, doubt kicked in as I trained for my first marathon. Running on the open highway, I asked God why I didn't know Dad was reading the Bible. *How come I didn't get to talk with him about You? How come when I tried to reach out to him, he didn't tell me? Why didn't I get to know all this?* "Is he really there with you, God?" I asked aloud, speaking into the air.

For whatever reason, maybe expecting an answer, I looked up—and it was then that I saw it. The cloud formation above me looked just like an angel. It had long wispy wings and a slender body. There was even a "dot" where a head would be. Stopping in my tracks, I stood there in awe. And then I felt the need to continue running. I ran the best I've ever run that day. My endurance was incredible, and I kept looking up to see if it was still there. And it was. It was as if it were following me, saying, "I'll always be with you. When you can't see me, I'll be in the wind." I was ecstatic.

However, like a roller coaster with its ups and downs, so goes the grief cycle. I crashed down about a month later. In the middle of the night, unbearable heartbreak and grief hit me and I knew I had to visit Dad's newly designated beach spot. I wanted to be close to my daddy. Since the memorial, I had not visited the beach spot, Dad's spot. Even though it was midnight, I decided to make the twenty-minute drive there. I went as I was, in sweatpants and sweatshirt, hair a mess from tossing and turning in bed all evening.

Leaving my purse in the car to avoid being mugged, I anxiously arrived at the bench Anne and I had sat on just one month earlier, saying goodbye to our father. The sound of the waves mesmerized me, and I sat and stared at the water, lost in the hum of the ocean.

"Want some?" I looked up to see a homeless man offering me the food in his hand. He looked about as scattered and askew as I felt.

"Oh, no, I'm good ..." I realized that he thought I too was homeless. "But thank you so much," I replied.

"No problem. We gotta take care of our own." He walked away.

The thought struck me that I should help him out. Running to my car and grabbing the money took about ten minutes and then I had to go find him. My worries of getting mugged were overshadowed by the idea of doing what Dad would've done. He would have helped the homeless man.

I found the man who had offered me food on a bench of his own, making a bed for himself.

"Hi ... I'm sorry to bug you, but I wanted to give you this." I held out the money.

Shaking his head, he said, "Oh, no, I don't take. I just give out here. I do appreciate ya, but I can't take that."

"But I insist. Please buy yourself a good meal tomorrow."

"No, ma'am. I can't take that from you." He turned his head away from me.

"Well, can I sit and talk with you?" *What am I thinking? This is crazy!* But something urged me on. I wanted to reach out my hand the way Dad did with Sal. I wanted to make an impact ... It would be Dad's legacy.

"I reckon you can." He turned back toward me, looking me up and down, probably wondering what my ulterior motive was.

Reaching my hand forward, I said, "Hi, I'm Abigail."

"Name's Earl. Nice to meet ya."

We sat for a few moments. The only sound was the ocean in front of us and the wind between us.

"What are you doing out here all by yourself? Are you on the street too?" Earl asked.

"No, I'm here because I couldn't sleep and I wanted to come to the spot where we recently spread my father's ashes. I just wanted to be with him, I suppose. Even though I'm not really with him … But you know what I mean."

"Yes, I do know. You know, I haven't always been this way." Illumination from the streetlights gave me a glimpse of his weather-beaten skin. *What a tough life this man must have lived.*

"How did you get here, Earl?" *Really, Abigail? Do you have no boundaries at all?*

"I was a businessman once, and I had a family. But I lost it all."

*Obviously he's an idiot alcoholic.*

"My family died in a car crash. It wasn't my fault; the car malfunctioned. But I can't seem to forgive myself." Raising his left hand, showing me his wedding ring, he said, "I can't let go, and they've been gone for six years. I've traveled the country trying to find peace. There is none. The closest thing to peace that I know is being out here where there are no limitations and no responsibilities. If I have nothing, nothing can be screwed up. They want to give me an insurance check, but how do I take money in exchange for my family?"

*This man is not drunk. Obviously, I'm the idiot.*

We talked for two hours, and both of us shared our pain and suffering from loss. We talked about how journaling and drawing were creative outlets that we both seemed to avoid … leaving us stuck in the pain. There were so many similarities between his life and mine. Between his life and

Dad's. He was a good man hammered down by life's blows. He was emotional and caring to a fault. He was artistic but didn't write and he no longer drew. Being stuck in life was the similarity between all three of our lives—Dad's, Earl's, and mine.

Every once in a while, he'd make a hand gesture that reminded me so much of my father. He'd hit his chest with his fist two times and make an *umph* sound. It was full of deep emotion and sort of an agreement with his soul, one that can't be expressed in words and which resonated through both of us.

"You'd better get going, girl." I knew he was right. I needed to get a few hours of sleep before work the next afternoon. "Can I walk you to your car?" he asked me.

That thing inside me, that wall of protection I hid behind for so long, had come down through this experience. I knew it wasn't wise to have him walk me to my car. I had parked in a well-lit area, but he still could easily hijack my car and/or do something worse.

"Sure, I'd like that," I heard myself saying. *What the ...?* Yet something felt safe about him.

"Thank you from the bottom of my heart for talking with me tonight. It's been years since I've had a real conversation with anyone. Most people out here are whacked out of their minds, and the ones who aren't are clever enough to take you for all you've got. You are a good friend and a good daughter. Thank you for being both to me tonight."

"Thank you, Earl. I hope you do what you promised me earlier. I hope you begin writing again. I wish I could check in on you to see if you have." *Give him your phone number.*

"Yeah, that would be cool. But it is what it is." He hopped up, and we started walking. We silently walked the mile to

27

the parking lot where my car was parked. Both of us were lost in our own thoughts, but it was a comfortable silence.

"Thanks for walking me, Earl. My car is just across the way there in the lot."

"I'll wait here, Abigail, and make sure you get in your car safely. I don't want anything to happen to you, and I want you to feel safe with me. So I'll wait right here, close enough to protect you if anyone comes up on you."

I walked to my car and grabbed a piece of paper. I wrote down my number and ran back over to him. With a shocked look on his face, he said, "What? You trust a complete stranger with your phone number?"

"Yes, I am going to trust you with my phone number. Just let me know that you are writing, okay? It's going to be an important part of your journey."

"Okay."

Two weeks later, there was a message on my answering machine. "Hey, this is Earl. If you can, meet me at your dad's spot tonight at sunset. I'll wait for you. I've got some big news." Ironically, I just so happened to be taking my daughter to a beach party close-by.

As I approached the bench, I saw his back. He was sitting and listening just as he had been that night I met him.

"Is that you, Earl?" I had not seen him during the daylight, so I wasn't sure if it was him.

When he turned, I almost dropped to my knees. The glow of the setting sun shimmered off his eyes. They were as soft and blue as my father's. It was like looking in Dad's eyes. With it being so dark the night we met, I had not seen this.

"Hey, you came! I can't believe it. You really did come to see me." His blue eyes filled with tears.

Still stunned by his eyes, I stepped toward him and sat

quietly next to him. I realized it was no small thing that he reminded me so much of Dad.

"So … hi. Yes, I wanted to hear your big news. Did you write? It sounded like great news on the message. What's up?"

"Well, yes, I have been journaling, but the great news is that I received my insurance payoff. I decided to call the attorney and accept it. Before, I didn't want to have the money because I saw it as blood money. But, Abigail, most importantly …" He paused and lifted his left hand. "My ring is in the ocean. I've chosen to forgive myself, and I choose to live again. My family will forever be with me. I've asked God to help me move forward. Knowing that, I have let go."

Feelings of elation and relief overcame me. I was ecstatic for Earl. We sat for a while and talked about the plans he had for his new life. He was going to go on a cruise and then go home to find a job and return to a more normal life. He invited me to go with him, but I graciously declined. It meant the world to me that he was going and that he was going to be okay.

"Abigail, hey, wake up …" The pastor's voice, along with a poke to my shoulder, brought me back to reality. Both he and Big Guy were standing above me, just looking down at me. Awkwardly, I jumped up and let the pastor into his seat. Once everyone was settled, there was silence and the thoughts ran through my head. *Did Big Guy hear my story as I was telling it to the pastor? Maybe he wasn't sleeping the whole time. Have others heard my story? They must think I'm crazy and a crazy storyteller.*

Big Guy popped in his earplugs, and his face was expressionless as he went back to his reading.

*Why do I care what he thinks? But the fact is that I do. Being looked down on because of my story is normal for me. I often feel, or assume, that people are going to judge me as being crazy. Big Guy's no exception.*

Several minutes went by before the pastor said, "I couldn't help thinking about everything you've told me so far, Abigail. I think you have quite an adventure ahead of you."

"Yeah, I guess so. I have no idea what to expect, so it'll be interesting to see how it all goes down. Maybe a jury member will give me answers."

"I hope that for you. Do you have a husband, and if so, what does he think?"

"No, no husband. I'm divorced and dating. I just met a guy who is pretty amazing and supportive of this journey of mine. He pursues me like I've never experienced. It's just one of the things taken from me—being pursued and wooed. It's just an innocent relationship, but I feel like the teenager who left town so many years ago … That's a whole other story for sure."

"Ah …"

It hit me that the hours we'd been on the plane were spent talking about me and my life and I knew nothing of him. "What about you? Where are you from? How many kids do you have?" I asked, switching the attention off myself for the first time during this flight.

"I have a boring life." He sighed. "But I am very content. I have been married to my best friend for twenty-one years, and we have three boys. We spend a lot of time being involved in the boys' sports. My wife is amazing, and I honestly don't know what I would do without her."

The rest of the flight was filled with light conversation about the pastor and his life. Deep down inside, I was jealous and felt regretful as I silently compared the trauma of my life to a seemingly normal life like his. I regretted so much of what I put my children through, and I wished I could go back and redo their childhood. If I could, I'd be a better mom. I'd put down all the how-to books and simply be more available and present with them.

Finally, it was time for us to deplane. We got our overhead bags and stood silently in line, the pastor behind me, and Big Guy in back of the pastor. We stood in silence waiting for the exit line to begin moving and as it did I realized I'd never even asked the pastor his name.

I turned back to him and said, "Hey, Pastor, I never got your name."

"When you write your book, just call me the man on the plane."

Big Guy looked back at me and nodded, giving me a huge smile.

# Chapter 4

# *Find the Beauty*

Stepping out the airport terminal and into the southern air, I paused. *Ahhhhh, I made it. I'm here.* The air feels different in the South; it is more refreshing, at least in November, when the humidity is low. I breathed it all in. The clean air filled my lungs, and the anticipation of seeing Kathy rejuvenated me. And then the anxiety hit. The idea of being in Little Mountain in a short couple of days caused my heart to pound, and I suddenly wanted to throw up.

"Ha, there you are!" I recognized my friend's voice and turned to see her running toward me. The anxiety turned back into excitement as we grabbed each other and hugged.

"I can't believe you're here!" she squealed.

"Me tooooo!" I squealed back.

Hugging me tightly she said, "Three years is way too long to go without seeing you, my friend! Not after spending every weekend together like we used to!"

That was what I loved about Kathy. She was always excited and happy to see me. She was positive and supportive. *Wait until she finds out what's in store for me after we work the wedding together!* I wondered how she was going to feel about why I was there … It wasn't just a work trip for me!

Diving right in, she asked, "So what's new? How are the kids? Are you dating? Fill me in, my friend!"

"The kids are good. They are so busy with school and their friends that I barely see them, and besides, they prefer to be at their dad's house. I'm accepting it more and more. As for dating, yes, I met this handsome guy and I like him a lot, but it's still so new still."

"What's he like? What's he do? Tell me everything!"

"Well, he's from Philly and is a total city guy. He works in construction." I fanned my face with my hand. "Yeah, he's hot." We leaned in and laughed together.

"Actually, Kath, there are some things I'm doing on this trip that I want you to know about. You know I'm going home to see my family. You know it's the first time in a long time … but I'm also going back to dig up the past." I lingered for just a moment before I continued, filling her in on the jury list and telling her of my plans.

"Wow! I am so proud of you, Abigail. I have always been blown away by your life story, and I can't wait to see what happens. I may not know all the details, but as I've told you before, Dean and I are totally here for you, no matter what you are going through. Whatever you need, really." Her heartfelt compassion was so authentic.

"Okay, so how are you and Dean doing?" I asked. "What's new with you guys?"

"Oh, we're good. It's the same ole, same ole." She chuckled. "We are boring. *Happy* and booooooring!" she exclaimed, and I felt pangs of jealousy.

"I'd take that kind of boring any day of the week, Kath." I looked out the window, taking in the city-like scenery with the old barns sitting right next to Starbucks.

Nashville is still country; it's just the big city kind of country—big enough that I don't feel as if I'm in the middle of God knows where but smaller than San Diego. The familiarity of the fast-food chain stores and a four-lane highway allow me to feel connected to the world still. But soon I'd be in God's country—you know, in the boonies. Nashville feels like a good transition. There is a hustle-bustle feeling here, yet I could still hide in this busy-enough city.

It was a short drive to Kathy and Dean's house. Once there, I unpacked and took a short nap, preparing myself for an evening of drinks and laughter with my friends. Tomorrow we would ride horses and have a healthy lunch before heading out to photograph the wedding.

Both Kathy and I were excited to work at the Country Music Hall of Fame, a first for us both. We spent the evening chatting as we went online and she showed me the places we were going to photograph the couple. The venue looked amazing, yet it was clouded by what was lying in the back of my mind.

It wouldn't be long before I *would* be entering God's Country, Little Mountain, Kentucky ... the real country ... my past. *If it's His Country, where was He then?*

The next day, the wedding went off without any problems, and as always, we had a blast working together. The venue didn't let us down, and being in downtown Nashville was a good middle ground place for me to be with all the thoughts swirling through my head.

Music was a constant as we walked the city streets, photographing, laughing, and creating beautiful images for the couple. The intimate interaction between the couple gave me hope.

Afterward, we couldn't wait to crawl into bed; wedding photography can be fun but exhausting!

Early in the morning, after a good night's rest, it was time for me to go. Shaking and nervous, I said goodbye to Kathy and Dean. I felt as if my life as I knew it, as unhealthy and uncomfortable as it seemed, was now over. I felt as though the events of the next few days could alter the trajectory of my life from here on out. It felt empowering and freeing but also unknown and uncertain.

With the music turned up, I drove down the interstate from Nashville and headed toward Little Mountain. Once off the main highway, I exchanged McDonald's and Starbucks for double-arched bridges and an occasional appearance of the Ten Commandments blaring on the billboards.

Eventually, I was alone, with the rolling hills of Kentucky and heading straight into the Bible Belt. There was a different church every two miles, and I wondered how many people actually went to these cute little chapels. The white steeple from each church against the blue sky was mesmerizing.

Rolling hills dotted with round bales of hay made by modern machinery were something I didn't remember. I recalled the stories my pop used to tell us about the bales of hay having been square and done by hand. Things had changed.

The abandoned barns resembled my heart, barely standing, as if the next wind could take them down. My thoughts hit as quickly as the cornrows whisking by. *What was I going to feel going into Little Mountain for the first time? Would it look the same? Would it feel the same? Would it smell the same? This place is home in my heart, and it's enemy territory. Would I see them? Would they see me and me not see them? Would they gang up on me? Would they ignore me? Would I ignore them?*

*Would I freeze in fear or fight in anger? It felt as if a million questions hit me at once.*

Too many thoughts were going through my mind at one time. Each negative thought felt like a prediction of what was about to happen, and I really didn't want to have any expectations at all, so I turned up the radio even louder to drown out the noise in my head.

The two hours it took to drive into my hometown felt like twenty hours, or a lifetime, but the *most* perfect song came on the radio as I turned off the two-lane highway, passing the "Welcome to Little Mountain" sign and onto Main Street.

*Hold on, to me as we go*
*As we roll down this unfamiliar road*
*And although this wave is stringing us along*
*Just know you're not alone*
*'Cause I'm going to make this place your home.*

Tears streamed down my face as I soaked up the lyrics, a small part of me believing them—the other part of me not so sure but praying they were true.

Regardless of my feelings, I had arrived home.

On the left was Harlan County School, one of two schools in this town. It had always confused me why there needed to be two schools in such a small town. The school Anne and I attended was Little Mountain Independent Schools, or LMS. *They* were the Harlan County Cardinals, and *we* were the LMS Trojans. The two schools were major rivals, which always confused me too. Why were we enemies when we lived in the same town?

Our alma mater's motto was "Go! Fight! Win!" The Cardinals wore all red, and we were "the blue and white."

Memories of the rivalry bombarded me, and surprisingly, the tears began. It was amazing how far away Harlan County School felt as a child. Through my child eyes and memory, the road to Harlan county School was a long road, in reality; it was a mere two miles away.

My heart started beating faster as I came up on the center of town where the *Doughboy* stood. It's a statue of a soldier who stands tall right in the middle of the town square. A boxed area across the bottom of the plaque contains an inscription:

For when the trumpets sound for Armageddon, only those
deserve undying praise who stand
where the danger is sorest.
—Theodore Roosevelt, 1918

A sense of reverence and awe overcame me, and I felt a bit like a warrior returning home.

Downtown Little Mountain is about six blocks long, and Pop, my grandfather, lived right in the middle of town, next door to the church I attended as a child, the church where I spent so much of my time and where I was baptized when I was nine—or perhaps ten.

Instead of going straight to Pop's, I decided to drive through the outskirts of town. I knew my way around because the roads were as familiar as if I had just left yesterday. Nothing had really changed, except the size of everything. It had all shrunk. What seemed like mansions to me back then were simple three-bedroom homes in reality.

I drove past all the homes we lived in as children. Miller's Grocery was in the center of the neighborhood I lived in. Its sign was now weathered and the building abandoned. It was at Miller's that I had discovered Moon

Pies and soda pop in glass bottles. Barefoot with my best friend, Elizabeth, I would walk from whatever apartment complex we lived in, as they were all close, and buy a Moon Pie and a bottle of Coca-Cola for twenty-five cents. Now it was boarded up. The park down the way had doubled in size. Turning the corner, I came upon the empty lot where all of us neighborhood kids played kickball. I could hear the laughter as my soul remembered so many fun times.

My journey through town ended at the shirt factory. It was the one building that seemed indifferent and unfamiliar to me. Yet my soul remembered this too. The last time I had been in that parking lot, it was early morning and still dark because the sun had not come up yet.

We were in an old gray beat-up car, and I remembered it was loud when it was running. He drove us into this very parking lot and turned off the ignition. With the car off, there was complete silence. My head and body were both numb with fear; all I could hear were the crickets. Rudy, the driver, interrupted the silence. "C'mon, girl, hop in the back seat. It's my turn."

Tears streamed down my face as I remembered my response so clearly. "No. I don't want to. I'm scared and need you to stop doing this to me."

"What do you mean, 'no'?" His expression was of true shock.

"Please take me home. I'm scared and … I'm sick." I begged him. I could still smell the stench of vomit from earlier in the morning. Or the nighttime … I didn't know what time it was or when I had thrown up all over the place. I just remembered being crouched over an old decrepit balcony of an unfamiliar house, afraid that the wood fencing would break, puking my brains out.

"Well, ain't that somethin'. I've waited all night for a piece of you. They got a piece of *that*, and I want some too."

I had been a piece of his three other friends' property all night long before they decided it was time for me to leave. Rudy had volunteered to take me home. Being in the car with just him, maybe because it was one against one, and not four against one, I felt as though I could fight for myself. I decided I would fight him if he touched me, but I was so tired that I wondered if I physically could.

He reached out to touch my hair, and the tears broke like a cracked dam giving way. The rush and flow of tears was unstoppable. Fear enveloped me. Through desperate sobs I muttered, "Please … take … me … home." Somehow that's all it took to convince him. He started the car, and it rumbled to life. As we pulled away from the shirt factory, the sun had begun to come up. There was light, and relief overwhelmed me in that moment. There was a real possibility of my nightmare finally being over.

Ten minutes later, I was safe at home. With my mom working the graveyard shift and my sister fast asleep, I was alone. I sat completely numb in a bathtub of scalding hot water, trying to wash the filth from my skin. I needed the water to enter me and cleanse the filth out of me as I forcefully pushed the water up and into my body with my own hand, trying to reach deep within myself. It didn't work that way, though. In the end, the filth had stuck to my soul.

And here I was so many years later, that same girl, having cleaned up on the inside a bit, but there was so much shame inside. I had cleaned up enough to be a functioning adult who had married and had children, but it was that filthy shame never being completely washed away that catapulted all my losses in life.

Leaving this town helped me ignore the problem and the

shame. The drugs and promiscuity, followed by a legalistic and over-spiritualized faith, had numbed me over the years. Being away from this town had kept me from facing the perpetrators, but in doing that, I had also run away from everyone I loved.

*I hate what they've done to me. I want to look them in the eyes! I want to put the blame where it goes! It's not me! I didn't do this. I want to face the people responsible for all this loss. But wait. Was that person me, this part of myself, the part that belonged here and never should have left, the one who went with the group that night?*

I felt the clash of who I was supposed to be with whom I actually was. But who was *that*? The discontent was uncomfortable, to say the least, yet the feelings of disassociation were welcomed and familiar to me. The wrestle was for acceptance of self. I was fighting a hard battle—one that I didn't feel equipped to fight.

Instead of running from the feelings of dissociation, I willed myself to sit still in it, the discomfort. It felt as though there were two girls in the driver's seat, completely divided against one another. But I—we—sat there in the parking lot of the shirt factory holding the jury list, waiting.

Finally, the grown-up won the inner battle. "Stop this, Abigail. You are okay." When I said it aloud to myself, I could pull myself out of the dissociative state. I took the jury list out of my bag and looking down at it, I wondered, *What will these people do to help me? Can they bring back what should have been? Isn't that what I want most, what should have been?*

"I don't know what to do with all this!" I screamed in the safety of my small rental car.

I was helpless and without answers, so I prayed. "God, I don't want to screw this up. I am not going through a door unless I know for sure that You have opened it. I don't know what to do from here, so You will need to make it completely obvious that it is You; and You will need to tell me exactly what to do here, because if You don't, I will screw it all up! I am knocking, God. Please answer."

It was getting late, and I knew Pop was waiting up for me. Reversing my car out of the parking spot, I whispered, "Seriously, God, I will mess this all up on my own. Lord, I need You."

During my earlier drive, most of the town was familiar and I felt a connection to the lost little girl that left so many years ago. Parallel to my life, the good memories were interrupted by the shirt factory and the ugly memories that went with it, but Pop's house would forever be the deepest connection to my childhood, a connection that would never be severed. The memories held it securely intact.

The door was open, and like so many years before, I didn't need to knock. I simply entered a safe and welcoming sanctuary called home. I belonged here. I always did. I knew he'd be sitting in his chair, and I knew he would say, "Well, look what the cat drug in!" I knew he would chuckle, and he didn't let me down. Pop was the most stable person in my life. He always had been. He never forced himself to be in my life, and just as I had with Dad, I had managed to push my grandparents away as well. Having occasional phone calls throughout the years certainly didn't replace the depth of connection of being together in the same room, feeling one another's presence.

Plopping into the living room chair, completely wiped out from my trip, I enjoyed the familiar smell of my grandparents' home and sighed with relief. My grandma's presence was still there, even though she had passed away ten years earlier and he had remarried Nilda, or Granny Nil, as we all called her. Granny Nil was fast asleep in the bedroom, but it wouldn't have mattered. Pop always spoke of my grandma when we talked. Even Granny Nil and I sometimes spoke of her during our short conversations on the phone. It wasn't awkward at all.

We fell into a comfortable conversation and then he asked, "Have you talked with Backer Worm?"

I laughed. He meant Leroy who as a child called tobacco worms, "backer worms". Leroy and I were each other's first crush in second grade, and our grandparents lived next door to each other throughout our childhood. We used to talk with each other over the fence. I have memories of him tattooed on my mind—and hand. The lead from a pencil is permanently tattooed into the palm of my hand from when we were in second grade and fighting over it. I won; however, I ended up stabbed, with the pencil lodged in my hand!

"No, Pop, I have not talked with Leroy." I snickered as the memory of my hand tattoo flooded me in that moment.

"Well, you get in touch with him while you're here. Call him." There was no questioning Pop when he spoke so sternly. He handed me the cordless phone. "Call him. He's a night owl."

"Um, okay." Not really having a choice, I looked up his name in the phone book and dialed the number.

A man answered on the first ring, giving me no time to change my mind. "*Hellllo.*"

"Is this Leroy Roth?" I asked, wondering if my voice sounded as shaky as it felt.

"Why, yeah. Who's this?" His voice sounded so … *country*.

"It's Abigail Blue, Leroy." Dead silence on the other end left me wondering if he remembered me. I held my breath and waited.

Finally, he said, "Well, I'll be ... Are you for real? Is this really you?" I suppose he did remember me!

"Yup, it's me, Abigail," I replied, my breath escaping my lungs. It had been over three decades since we'd talked.

"Well, where you been, girl? How are ya?"

"I've been in California. I'm ... good. I'm home and at Pop's right now. How are you, Leroy? What have you been up to?"

"For thirty years ya been in California? Oh myyyyy God. I can't believe I am talking to you. You're really at your pop's, at Hank's?"

"Yes, I am. I'm only here for a couple of days. How are you?"

"I'm fine. I'm fine. What have I been up to? Good Lord, girl, it's been so long, where would I begin. Hmm ... Well, I'm just so tickled to be talkin' to ya. I work with my dad as a land assessor and worked as a detective before that."

My interest was piqued. A detective? *Could it be that Leroy can help me since he's a detective? Okay, Lord, if this is an open door, I want to walk through it. But you have to be obvious, God.*

"I'd love to see you while I'm here." *What? Did I just say that?*

"I'll pick ya up from Hank's—I mean Pop's—tomorrow and we'll go have lunch. Does that work for ya?" he asked.

"Yes, that's perfect."

"I'll see ya tomorrow at noon." And that was it. It didn't feel like anything I should have been afraid of. He was welcoming and didn't reject me as I had expected.

When I glanced over at Pop, he winked as I shook my head and sighed. "I think I'm home, Pop. I think I'm finally home." I closed my eyes and laid my head back on the chair's headrest.

Abbey M. Blue

We spent the rest of the evening talking about the kids and the farm and Granny Nil's upcoming retirement. She had been working part time at the Walmart for years and was finding that it was too much for her.

I heard all the army stories I grew up hearing about, and just like when I was a child, I didn't understand half of them, but I was mesmerized with my pop and the honor that exuded from him. When Pop told a story, there was always a lesson to be learned. As he spoke, I was captivated not by the details but by his mannerisms and how familiar they were to me, even though it had been many years since I'd seen him.

The next morning, I woke up nervous about seeing Leroy, but all my apprehensions were alleviated the moment I got into his car. First off, he hadn't changed a bit; he was exactly as I remembered him. His big puppy dog hazel eyes and that silly crooked smile put me at ease as soon as I got into his car. Even after all this time, he was still familiar to me, and I instantly relaxed, feeling safe. Still, I didn't want to lead the conversation. I wanted God to, through Leroy. I had to be open to the idea that we would discuss small talk to keep things on the surface. It didn't take long for me to realize we were going deep.

"Well, girl, the first thing I gotta say is where did ya go and why'd ya leave without any heads-up?" He turned to me, taking his eyes off the road for just a brief moment and looked me straight in the eyes.

"I couldn't take it anymore, Leroy. After everything happened, I had to get out of town." My eyes shifted downward, and I noticed how clean his car was. I almost missed the shock in his voice.

"After what happened?" We locked eyes as he said it.

"You know, the stuff that happened to me. Don't make

44

me say it." I felt embarrassed at the idea of giving the details after all this time.

"I have no idea what you're talking about. I don't know what happened to you. I just know that my friend was there one day and gone the next. I had no idea where you even went." He seemed sincere, but was he messing with my head? How could he have not known? *Everyone* knew.

Glancing over at me again, he quietly asked, "Why did you leave here, Abigail?"

It was then that I realized that he truly didn't know why I had left town so many years ago. I knew that I would have to tell the story to him and explain more than I was prepared to talk about. The thought never occurred to me that anyone in this town did *not* know. I had lived with a stigma as the town slut for over thirty years. Something in me stirred, and anger, on top of deep loss, hit me all at the same time. I felt robbed all over again.

I didn't know how to answer his question. "I'll explain it over lunch, okay?" I answered. At least I had a few minutes more of driving to gain the courage to tell the story.

That time came within ten minutes, as we sat at the table across from each other. I told him of the rape and the trial and the bullying from the boys' girlfriends' at school ... and the shutdown of my soul. I told him how I just went *blank* at a certain point with shame and self-blame bigger than I was. With each word, I became more and more shocked over the fact that he didn't know. For all these years, in my mind, all my friends knowing and judging me, giving me the public humiliation as that of the town slut, defined a large part of the perception of myself. It was one of the roots of my shame. The same shame I had been carrying for decades, the shame so familiar to me, was, what ... false?

If Leroy didn't know that meant, he had never judged

me. What about the other friends that I had walked away from? Confusion tore through me like a tornado over one of those old barns that I'd passed on my way here, finally blowing it over. I felt like one of those dilapidated structures, internally falling into a pile of rubble.

I don't think Leroy knows, even to this day, how much what he said next meant to me. "Abigail, had we all known, you'd have had an army behind ya. I am soooo sorry you have dealt with this for all these years. We just didn't know, girl." He spoke for our circle of friends. He spoke for the children who, only kids at the time, had created a foundation of structure and identity together.

He spoke to the part of me that never wanted to leave and wished she never did. The circle was broken for me when I left. Every single thing I had ever lost due to this crime came rushing in on me. The memories felt so unbearable, and yet I just sat there. I was composed on the outside, but the internal storm of emotions his words unleashed battered my soul.

The tears started when he said, "So what do you want me to do? How can I help? Tell me who and I'll take a baseball bat to their heads and then justice will finally be had." I wasn't used to someone wanting to fight *for* me. Not that I ever wanted violence, and still don't, but there was something in the intention of it that touched me so deeply— as I was on his team and he was literally ready to go to bat for me. He was willing to protect and fight for me.

"That's not what I want. I want to know why ... and ... I want to look at least one of them in the eyes. I want to face them and stop finding the perp in the mirror. I need to finally put the blame where it belongs." I knew even back then as I said the words that that wasn't what was going to free me, but it sure felt like a good place to start.

"A bat to the head would be a lot easier. Can't I just do that?" Leroy was trying to bring humor into the conversation.

"No, I have something I want to show you, and maybe that will make it easier."

Leroy's face was hard to define as I showed him the court administrative paperwork and the jury list. His eyes skimmed the paperwork, and he kept saying, "Wow." As he discovered who the real characters in my story were, I thought I saw him wince.

He knew the people, and it startled me when he told me where I could find one of the jury members. He knew where she worked. He also told me that he had previously worked for the judge who was my attorney at the time.

"I can help you, Abigail, and I want to. What do you want me to do?" he asked.

"I don't know what to do. I think what I want is to talk to any jury members who I can and ask why I wasn't believed. I want to find out where the boys live and simply look at them and then walk away. Can you help me with that?" My whole body was inwardly shaking, yet somehow I was still outwardly composed.

"Why yeah, I can do that. I'll go back to my office and see what I can find out." He handed the paperwork back to me and hesitated. "Can I make photocopies of these papers?"

Fear struck me, but I felt I could trust him. "How about I go with you and you photocopy them while I'm there?" And then I explained why I was so afraid of letting them out of my presence.

"These papers have been in my possession since the day I received them. I have always known where they were. I have guarded them with my life and the idea of them being out of my possession for even a moment gives me anxiety." I sounded so desperate. I suppose I was.

"Let's go," he said as he led me out the door with his arm around my shoulder.

## ~Careful Where You Walk~

After lunch and visiting Leroy's office to make copies, I returned to Pop's house and sat alone on the front swing of the porch. The inability to swing it out this time was most evident.

So much had just happened. Who knew that coming here would have turned out like this? Never would I have thought that people in this town didn't know about the public disgrace that kept me away from home for so long. Devastated, I didn't know what to do or who to talk to, but I needed to talk!

Grandma would have had the answers. Grandma was up front and to the point. As a child, she always brought clarity to any problems I had. She would have cleared things up for me if she were here. I envisioned what it would be like to have a heart-to-heart talk with her and ask her advice. I wondered what it would have been like to receive advice from her about this. I didn't recall ever talking with my grandparents about the rape, or the trial for that matter, and as an adult, I never got to know her.

I was thirteen when I left here, and all of a sudden, I missed her like never before. I imagined that she would be practical and to the point in her answer for me. Wishing I could be with her, I realized I had not been to her gravesite and that it was time.

Have you ever noticed how carefully you have to walk in a cemetery? They say you are being disrespectful if you walk where the dead are lying. They, the live folks, are more concerned about it than the ones resting ever so peacefully. I mean do they (the dead ones) really care? I think if anything, they are happy you are there visiting.

There isn't a square inch of a countryside cemetery open for walking. Each step I take must've been pissing somebody off. But I made my way to Grandma's gravesite without having an absolute panic attack. She had been lying there for ten years, and this was my first time visiting her. Add to my list of things stolen: visiting Grandma.

*How did I let my hometown get stolen from me? On top of my childhood? Do I hate you? Do I forgive you? Who am I really directing these questions to? The perps, the people I thought judged me, my parents ... my grandparents ... myself?*

Anyway, back to Grandma. I sat right there on the ground over her, on top of her, and spoke to her. *They must really think I'm nuts.*

"What do I do with all this information, Grandma? Do I take advantage of this list I hold in my hand? I don't know if I should contact jury members or let it all go. What would you tell me to do?" I began to weep because I couldn't get any real answers from the grave. I wept because I actually expected an answer to miraculously appear in front of me.

"I think you'd tell me to forget about it all—or maybe not." I didn't know what she would tell me because I never really got to know her wisdom. Frustrated, I got up, upset that I wouldn't get answers this time. I expected that if I asked, God would answer. I was asking Grandma, but deep down, I was expecting Him to answer. *I guess have to figure this one out on my own.*

I walked to the other side of the tombstone and fell to my knees when I read the unexpected inscription printed on the opposite side:

> *Persistence is to man as carbon is to steel. Look forward with enthusiasm and backward with pleasure.*

There it was, even though I had no idea what carbon was to steel, I knew persistence was my answer. I needed to persist with the information that I had and try to find out what I could. Only then could I let it go and move forward.

What I had wanted earlier while swinging and wondering what Grandma would advise me to do was right in front of me—and the answer was as straightforward as I imagined it would be.

~Love, Mom~

Who knows if it is even legal to call up a person who sat on a jury of a court case from thirty years ago where you were the victim who didn't get the justice you sought, but that is exactly what I did as soon as I left Grandma's grave and went back to Pop's house. The house was empty, everyone having gone to the store.

The phone book was about one-fourth inch thick for the whole town, and it didn't take me long to search all the names from my coveted jury list. It was surprising to find that there was only one person from the jury list in the phone book.

Dialing the number with shaky hands, I half hoped she wouldn't answer. But she did. She was an older woman, and she said she didn't remember ever being on a jury. She insisted about that repeatedly. I asked her to think hard to try to remember, but I knew quickly that I wasn't going to get anywhere with her. It was odd how she kept me on the phone, though.

"But, honey, how are you? And how is your life? Where have you been, and what have you been doing all these years? Are you okay? Have you been okay?"

As I answered all her questions, I was reassuring her and that's not what this was meant to be! *I* wanted to ask the questions; *I* wanted to get the answers. But, that's not how it went. The conversation ended by giving her my phone number and asking her to call me if she remembered anything someday. I knew I'd never hear from her again, and in the end, I never did.

I would only speak to one more juror, the one that Leroy had told me about, mentioning that she worked at the local grocery store. It only took ten minutes to drive there, and nervously I walked around the store until I worked up enough courage and asked for her at the customer service counter.

She was on her lunch break, and because I didn't think I could stand another hour in the public spotlight, I left my business card along with a note in a sealed envelope for her. On my note, I explained that I was part of a court case in 1981 for which I believed she had been a jury member. I expressed that it would mean the world to me if she would call me back and answer a couple of my questions.

I didn't think I'd hear from her, but two days later, I was surprised to answer my phone and find out is was her! She did the same thing as the other juror, asking me a bunch of questions, and when she was done getting her answers, she denied ever being on a jury. *Why did she even call me back?*

The jury list had proven to be for naught. I had no answers from it, just more questions. *Why did these two women care about my life? Why did they ask about me with so much care and concern? Was it true Southern hospitality or perhaps a bit of remorse and curiosity?*

And that was it. There would be no more phone calls and no more questions for jury members. Exhaustion and despair overcame me, and I needed to shut myself away from it all and not remain in Little Mountain anymore. The friends I thought had judged me for these three long decades didn't judge me, yet they also couldn't understand my pain. And the ones who were supposed to know about it, the jury members, denied it outright. Their denial fed into the pain that was beginning to surface. Could anyone answer my lifelong question of *why?* Why was it so hard to get someone to acknowledge my pain? Was I the only person aware of it? It seemed to be something only I could see.

At Pop's, I sat down on the living room floor. There was something about this living room that comforted me. It was my safe place as a kid. It was the place I ran to after a hard day at school. I'd plop down right in this same exact spot and sit mesmerized watching *Batman*. I couldn't get here fast enough those days. The anticipation of a spotlight appearance of Batgirl was enough to make me skip playing with my friends. Oh, how I loved Batgirl! She had power and was clever. She warded off the bad guys, and she was the sidekick to Batman. She was my hero, but they didn't have her on the show often. Her character was short-lived. If she wasn't on, at least I could see Catwoman. She was sexy and conniving. She was thrilling, and even though she was the enemy, I loved her. I sat starry-eyed with every one of her performances.

Those were the good ole days, when I didn't have anything to run from. Life was good. Grandma was always there when I got home from school, and she let me just be myself. She seemed to always make a way for me to get out of gardening because she knew I was allergic and got headaches.

Of course, Pop thought it was nonsense and that I should be working, but Grandma knew the truth and allowed me to instead dust the living room or help her clean the house. She kept the chore list short and allowed me to get my *Batman* time in. Grandma and I had an understanding. I believe she understood me better than I did. She was always quiet about it and never did she show any outward expressions of love … I just understood that she had a deep love for me by the way she treated me.

The screen door slammed and woke me up from my daydream, bringing me back to reality.

"Hey, what you doin'?" Anne, my sister, came in like a hurricane, carrying an arm full of grocery bags. Anne's get 'er done personality always did just that … got things done. She had come over to make lunch for us all. The plan was to have a nice lunch and then do some porch sittin', a much-loved country "sport." Porch sittin' is bonding time.

"Here, let me grab that for you, Anne. What did you bring?"

"Well, I just brought some lunchmeat and stuff from Piggly Wiggly. I'll go put it away. Here, this bag is for you." She handed me a grocery bag with a bunch of papers in it and continued to the kitchen, leaving me alone in the living room again.

She yelled to me from the kitchen, "I was cleaning out my closet and came across these old letters addressed to you! There's a bunch of old pictures of the kids in there too. You'll want to go through them all."

"Okay, thanks." I peeked into the bag and saw letters addressed to me from my mother. My attention was immediately piqued. "Where did you get these, Anne?" I asked in the direction of the kitchen. My eyes were fixated on the handwriting of my mother on the envelopes. I didn't remember any letters from my mom.

"I told you. In my closet, in a box. I have no idea what's in there. I just saw your name and thought I'd let you sort through them," she called back.

Immediately I grabbed one of the envelopes and opened it. It was dated May 18, 1981, one month after I left town. I expected the letter to be superficial—that's what I knew of my mom for all these years but I was completely taken aback when I read it.

> *Dear Abigail,*
>
> *How are you? Was glad to hear you made it safe and sound to your dad's. Write and tell me about your trip.*
>
> *I talked to Anne last night, and she is feeling better. She goes back to the doctor tomorrow for a checkup.*
>
> *I know you are hurting and only time will heal that hurt. I know you will pull out of this whole mess. As hard as it is, try to put it out of your mind and start a new beginning. I know you can. Eventually, maybe you and Elizabeth can write each other with no hard feelings. I hope so.*
>
> *One thing I would like to say is* don't ever consider yourself a "whore," *as you put it. You are one fantastic lady in my book, no matter what has happened. Remember what I told you about love? What happened to you happens to many young ladies. What makes you so special*

*is you had the courage to bring it out in court, and I will always admire that courage.*

*I remember telling you, "Someday a young man will come along and love you and you will love him. Love is a giving and sharing between two people." When that time comes for you, you will know it. You will always be tops with me. Anytime I can help you, let me know. I will do my best. If you have a problem you feel you can't cope with alone, your dad and Dee love you too and I know you can always confide in them. Don't ever break the love they have for you. Don't be bashful to confide in them. Remember that they, like myself, are always willing to listen. If you need to get in touch with me you can always call work and leave a message for me to call you back. If you ever need to, call me collect.*

*From here on, just tell yourself, "I'm number one (with pride) and make a new start. After all you've been through, I know you will be all right.*

*As far as not wanting to come back to Kentucky, I understand your feelings—believe me. One day you may change your mind, but whatever you decide will be all right with me, okay?*

*Well, as far as news around here ...*

How did I *not* remember any of this? She told me to focus on love, hold my head up high, and live a good life, put it all behind me and move on. My eyes were going faster than my brain could take it in. Why is my memory that of not talking with my mother for five years? Why do I feel as if things were never talked about, yet here were the words to prove they were? My brain was quickly realizing that my perceptions of what I thought happened were a bit different from what actually happened.

So far, my friends haven't judged me the way I thought they had and my mother didn't just send me away with no emotion or thought of me. She didn't disregard me and send me away. She thought she was giving me a better life. But why didn't she go with me? Why didn't she make a better life *with* me? Why stay here all these years—without me? The familiar feelings of unworthiness washed over me, and I couldn't make sense of the pull happening inside me. *Who am I?*

The part Mom mentioned about Elizabeth was confusing. I had blurry memories of the trial and the three months preceding it. I knew that Elizabeth and I had not spoken since but I couldn't remember what exactly had happened. How could I block so much out? Elizabeth and I were the best of friends before it all had happened.

The feelings of shock in how this trip was turning out hit me all over again. I thought my journey to justice would involve answers from the jury members, and I simply did not expect to be reading my mother's thoughts from so many years ago. I just wanted to stand tall and proud and look injustice in the eye. Instead, I was leaving tomorrow with more questions and new feelings that felt like a tornado churning inside, threatening to destroy what was in its path: my heart and soul.

Luckily, there wasn't much time to ponder these things. I had to pull myself together for some porch sittin' because Pop and Granny Nil had returned from the store and Anne had lunch all ready for us. Despite the stormy weather inside me, we enjoyed our lunch as we hung out on the porch.

The conversation was calm and peaceful, but it was hard to concentrate and hold back the tidal wave of emotions about to surface. It wasn't until later that evening when I was alone with the letters that I sobbed my heart out and allowed the dam to break.

The child in me who had been in need of a mother for so many years softly read the words aloud. I read to myself, and my whole self *listened*.

The survivor in me probably had no way of knowing how to hear my mother's words back then. I was in survival mode, shutting anything potentially harmful out. I was sitting here now as a mother who had made so many mistakes of her own, mistakes that left my children having to get through life sometimes *without their mother*.

In the letter, my mother expressed her belief that if I lived with my dad, I'd have a better life. *She wanted me to have a good life*. I sat still on that bottom bunk bed where my heart met hers, and something in me awakened.

I could completely understand the desire to give my child a better life. During the times in my children's lives that I was not the best parent for them, I had to allow their dad to take over. I wanted what was best for them.

My heart was awakened but a heavy fatigue came over me as I sat amongst the fragmented pieces of motherhood.

# Chapter 5

# *Going Gilgal*

When a couple begins dating, they are often advised to avoid sharing too much too soon, yet there we were, home in San Diego, sitting in the park, going against all the rules that *they* say are taboo.

Matt sat across from me as I filled him in on every detail of my trip. When I was excited, I could see him perk up; when I was sad and tears welled up in my eyes, his welled up too. He may not have completely understood, but his care for me was evident. In the moments when he wasn't reciprocating emotion and I thought I had lost him, he'd say just the right thing, letting me know he was in it with me.

Or was he just flattering me?

Doubt crept in, and by the time his lunch break was over, I was convinced that I'd never see him again. I mean, he seriously had to think I was crazy.

When he didn't call for a few days, I gave him the benefit of the doubt that maybe he was just busy with work. When he didn't call for ten days, I was convinced that it was over before it had even begun.

The impact of this weighed heavily on me and almost

derailed me. I had his support three weeks ago for the first trip back, and here I was getting ready to return for the second scheduled trip back—and I had to do it on my own.

I was tired of doing things alone.

Facing my past felt like a big wound, one so big that when Leroy e-mailed to tell me that he had an address for one of my rapists, I wasn't sure I could face him.

The anxiety lingered over the next week, and then it grew. And grew. And grew. I envisioned going to his house, knocking on his door, and ... what? Yes, I would look at him eye-to-eye, but then what? Would I want to punch him? Would he want to punch me?

Even though I flew on the same airline and took the same flight as I had three weeks earlier, this flight was much different. I didn't have the blessing of having a pastor sitting beside me. I was alone with my thoughts, but instead of dwelling in the negative, I spent the whole flight trying to catch up on the Bible study I was doing at church. The current chapter was about the timeline of Israel, and as interesting as the Promised Land was to learn about, I couldn't really concentrate.

It was the first time I'd studied the Promised Land, and it was intriguing. Until now, I was way behind on the study and had planned on getting caught up on the plane, but I just couldn't get into it. My thoughts were filled with what was going to happen the next day. I had an address that could be Graham Broderick, one of the rapists, and come tomorrow; I could be looking him in the eye. He was the one I had full recollection of from that awful night oh so long ago.

Relief hit me in knowing that I didn't have to be a "professional" until next week, when I would be working at a wedding with Kathy! I just needed to make it through the next few days and hopefully enjoy Kathy and Dean's bed-and-breakfast–style home in peace!

By the time I arrived in Nashville and saw Kathy, it was physically evident that I was in full panic attack mode. My hands were shaky, and I couldn't keep my neck still. The spasms were overwhelming, and Kathy noticed it right away.

"Abigail, you are a mess. Do you take anything for your anxiety? Can I do anything for you?" she asked. I shook my head. "Ya know, Dean can do some hypnosis with you and help you. Think about it, okay?" she said, love in her tone. I knew Dean was a hypnotherapist, but I never thought anything like that could work on me. Maybe others, but not me!

I couldn't imagine being able to be hypnotized, because I doubted I could relinquish that sort of control to another person. I needed whatever control I had left in my life.

When I arrived at their house, Dean immediately noticed my panic. He offered to meditate with me. I told him I couldn't do hypnosis but that I would do relaxation meditation, and we headed to the yoga room that was his workspace. He called it 'timeline therapy', and I thought of the word "timeline" that was in my Bible study of Israel and the Promised Land.

Was there a connection here that I needed to pay attention to?

Dean is a patient, caring, loving, and gentle man. I knew him to be safe and trustworthy. So much so, that being in the room with him and opening myself up without Kathy there was not so much a miracle, but a great example of the fact that I felt safe with a man.

"Sit wherever you want. Get comfy," he said. I sat on the ground floor and leaned back against the wall; the thick new carpet under me was comforting. The room itself had high-beamed ceilings and all white walls, giving me a solid sense of peace.

Opposite of where I sat was a piano, and I drifted off in my mind, wondering why I never learned the piano. I had always wanted to. I focused on the piano, nervously adjusting and readjusting my sitting position.

"Okay, Abigail, this isn't hypnosis," he reassured me, "and it is not going to take you out of control." My sense of trusting him heightened because he "got me."

"You will actually have a very acute awareness of everything we are doing, more so than usual. We can stop at anytime. We will start with breathing and trying to get you somewhat relaxed, and then I will guide you with my words into some imagery and see where it takes us. Know that you are the one that is in complete control of this."

"I'm afraid I'm doing something wrong ... spiritually," I said, tears welling up. I was so desperate for relief and help, and Dean seemed so trustworthy, but still, I didn't want to lose my faith in the process. I lowered my head and prayed silently for God to speak. *Is this okay, Lord. It feels okay—I feel peace in trying this—but can you please protect me if it isn't?*

Dean began the process, and within minutes, I was relaxed and breathing slow, deep breaths. He had me envision what I wanted my life to look like in twenty-five years. What would I be doing? How did I look? I didn't see anything. We went to fifteen years from now and then to five years from the present. I still couldn't see much. It was too blurry to envision a future. We skipped the present, and he asked me to envision myself as a small child. The little girl was riding her bike and chewing gum, smiling big, as if she had no cares at all in the world. Her pigtails bounced back and forth as the wind blew across her face.

Next I heard him ask me to go to the time right before

the traumatic event in my life, and while my heart started beating faster just thinking about the rape, I was able to sort of skip past it in my mind and jump to a memory that was right before the incident. I saw myself and a boy who had a crush on me at that time. We were hanging out with a bunch of other friends at the skating rink. He had pulled me aside and was kissing me. I was telling him to stop because it was too much. I wasn't ready for that, and I walked away from him.

Dean's voice interrupted the memory, but not before I realized that I had said *no*! I had told him no! It was a power I never knew I had.

"Okay, Abigail, now let's go to the traumatic event in your life. You don't need to tell me what you see. This is for you."

Immediately I was on a bed, probably the bed I was raped on, and there were two parts of me. There was a line straight down the middle of my body, separating me in half. The right side of my body was completely black, and the left side was normal. I could see my eyes, my hair, my clothes, all fully intact, but only on the left side of my body. I suppose I disconnected during that traumatic event. I could feel the tears on my face and the carpet under my body, but I felt so different. I felt light and airy, and I attempted to explain what I was seeing. I wanted help in remembering this later, if nothing else.

"I want you to hover over this part of your timeline, Abigail," Dean whispered. "Just stay over it and don't run. Do you maybe have a gift for her?" he asked.

"I don't know what to give her," I replied. I didn't know what she needed. Instantly I had a picture of my oldest daughter, and I knew what I'd do if she were lying there, I'd hug her, hold her, and not let go. I went to the bed and hugged my smaller self. It was not my daughter lying there. It was me. I could feel the familiarity of being a little girl, something that had been gone for so many years. It was then that I had the overwhelming urge to protect her. I, Abigail, the adult self, wanted to protect Abbey, my inner little girl self.

"Does she have something to give you?" I heard Dean faintly say from a distance. The more I connected with her, the more distant his voice became. She handed me a circle. I mean, it looked like what I thought was a clear glass ball.

Warmth instantly filled me. Forgiveness warms. Forgiveness softens. Forgiveness renews and empowers. Forgiveness reconnected us in that very moment. I felt whole and complete, yet in that moment, I knew there was so much more to come. I had the assurance that things were going to get better and more complete between us, the little girl I was and the woman I had become.

It was so moving, and I wanted it to stay this way forever. I knew I was ready to come out of the session.

"I'm ready, Dean. I'm done."

"Okay, wonderful," he said. "Let's bring you back to the present with her. Can you hold hands with her as you both get off the bed? Could you help her up and look around the room? What do you see?"

"There's a door to my left," I replied, relieved. Doors were good.

"Go toward the door. Open it and walk out of the room."

As we got up off the bed, I grabbed her hand and she looked up at me. She paused and sat there. She was happy, but I could see weariness in her eyes. She'd been waiting a long time for this. She grabbed my hand and smiled the sweetest smile I'd ever seen. *Let's go.* And we walked toward and out the door.

As I traveled from the distant past and back into the present-day reality of the yoga room, the piano was the first thing I saw and heard. Dean was sitting at the piano, and he was playing a sweet and precious melody. Tears drenched my face as I sat and listened. When the song was done, he came over to me and kneeled in front of me.

"I want to ask your permission to pray over you, Abigail. Is it okay if I pray in the name of Jesus, asking the Holy Spirit to seal the work He has done here?" Dean's eyes were full of compassion. I nodded my head, signaling yes. After praying a beautiful prayer over me, Dean suggested that I go to my room and hang out with myself and marinate in what had just taken place. It was a precious gift to be guided so beautifully by my friend. The really amazing part of it all is that Dean and Kathy are not Christian. Dean was honoring my faith in everything he was doing with me.

As I lay there on the bed, reveling in the beauty of the healing, I prayed my own prayer. I prayed that I wouldn't wake up without her, that we wouldn't disconnect in my sleep.

Waking up "whole" was exciting. I had fallen asleep with the expectation that the special effect would wear off as I slept and I'd be back to the icky dissociated state I was so familiar with. But it wasn't like that at all. My eyes opened, and I knew it was still different. I was still different; I was healing on a much deeper level than ever before.

After packing and saying my good-byes to my dear friends, I was off and on my way to Little Mountain, where I would be (if all went as planned) facing my biggest enemy. I thought hard about what to do next. I mean, if I had been healed or something, did I even need to go and search out this man who had hurt me? *Did I still need to look him in the eyes?* Perhaps the main reason I came here this time was to find myself, and hadn't that happened during meditation? I decided I would pursue it. If I didn't at least try, I'd probably go home regretting it and always wondering what would have happened.

While I drove along the countryside, I made a pact with God that if I didn't get to see him/any of them face to face, I'd let that part go.

I could not get the circle I had been given the night before out of my head. Stopping at the few Christmas stores along the way, trying to find an empty snow globe, I got excited. However, all I found were Christmas globes, and I wanted an empty one. I wanted a circle. I envisioned handing that same circle of forgiveness over to my enemy.

Unfortunately, I didn't find it. No store had that kind of circle.

The address was easy to find. My heart beat wildly as I turned onto his street. When I found the number, I drove past a couple of times before stopping. The house was a one-story Craftsmen-style home that was my favorite type of home and the kind I had always hoped to buy one day. It had a wraparound porch and a new barn in the back. As injustice would have it, he appeared to have the things I had always wanted.

There weren't any cars parked in the driveway, so I pulled in and parked. My nerves were surprisingly calm at this point, and I didn't hesitate to get out of the car. I walked up the porch steps and rang the doorbell. By the door was a UPS package that had been delivered. It had his name on it.

My heart raced for a moment at the sight of his name. Had I *found* him? Or was this someone else's house with the same name?

I rang the bell three times, with no response. If I had found him, he wasn't here. No one was. I didn't know what I would have even said if someone else had answered the door, and that is when it really hit me. *What if he has children and a normal life now? What if he turned out to be a good guy and had a good life with good people in it? What if my presence messed up those other good people?*

I knew in my heart of hearts that it was time to turn around and go. I knew there was nothing to say or do. The night before, I had found the piece of myself that had been taken from me. I was whole again, and that wholeness was something I didn't want to be in his presence. *Could the very sight of him break me in two once again?*

Taking one more chance at seeing what his life was like, I peeked inside the window of the door. There, on a small table in the middle of the foyer, was a photograph of a couple. I leaned my forehead against the glass as the air left my lungs, staring at the photograph.

The man and woman looked back at me from the photograph. The man fit the description of how I remembered him—blond hair and blue eyes. The blue eyes stared straight through me. I *had* what I wanted: eye-to-eye contact. I stared back, and in that moment, I surrendered the burden of responsibility to him.

Still against the glass on the door, I said softly, "You hurt me. You really hurt me. You took a piece of me that was not yours. You violated me and *you* broke me into pieces."

The emotion I felt was unexpected. Not because of its intensity—quite the opposite. It was solid, secure, and just matter-of-fact, simple and so peaceful. I felt the warmth of forgiveness wash over me. I closed my eyes and pictured myself giving him the circle. I couldn't envision anything more than that. I couldn't see if he received the circle. I could only see myself giving it to him. As quickly as it happened, it ended. The image was gone, and it was time to go.

I didn't look in the rearview mirror as I drove away.

All those years ago, when I moved to California, Mom moved to the neighboring town of Alba, a mere twenty minutes from Little Mountain. I decided to drive there.

It's an unfamiliar town because Mom lived here, not me. It was not home or even remotely familiar to me at all. Not wanting to see anyone just yet, I decided to walk through downtown Alba. I circled through the foreign-to-me town a couple of times, not knowing where to go because it looked abandoned. I parked at the bank on the south end of town and walked north, through the tiny village of aged brick buildings, mostly vacant with "Out of Business" signs displayed. Many of the structures were going to fall down at any moment, based on their looks.

The ringing of my cell phone startled me, and Leroy's name appeared on my screen.

"Hey there," I answered.

"Hey, girl, what's up? Did you go?" Leroy asked, his tone curious.

"Yes, I did. Thank you so much for providing the address, Leroy. It means a lot to me. I went to the address, and it was his house. A package was there with his name on it, but no one was home," I said, hearing my own emotionless tone as if I were a foreigner to myself.

"I'm sorry you didn't get to see him in person. I know that was important to you." His tone was pained.

"No, no, it was actually perfect. I saw his photograph through the window and looked into his eyes ... and well ... that was good enough for me. Thank you so much!"

"Wow! Okay. I'm glad that I could help!" He enthusiastically asked, "Now what?" Turning the corner, I stopped walking. I didn't know what was next.

"I have no idea." Just as I had said the words I recognized

the name on the window sign in front of me. Lovell's Law Offices. "Wait. Leroy, is Jeston Lovell's office in Alba? I'm standing in front of his office if it is!"

"Yup, he's in Alba. Ring the bell and go on in and see him," he stated, his country twang giving me courage, but not enough.

"I can't do that; I'll need an appointment, won't I?"

"You ain't in California no more, girl. Ring the bell," he insisted with a chuckle.

"Ummmm, okay. Wow, what do I say?" I fumbled with my words. "This is crazy. Okay, here I go!"

"Good luck," he said right before hanging up, leaving me staring at the office door in front of me. To the right of the office door was the bell. I rang it and waited. At first, I didn't think anyone was going to answer, but then a crackled "Yes?" came from the voice box on the outside cobblestone wall.

"Hi, I'm hoping I can talk with Mr. Lovell," I said unsurely.

"Okay, but who are ya?" the speaker screamed back at me.

"My name is Abigail Blue, and I'm an old client of Mr. Lovell's. I'm sure he won't remember me, but I'm hoping to talk with him about my old case." I managed to get that much out.

"Door's open. Come on in."

*I'm certainly not in California. I'd have to call to make an appointment and hope to get in within the next month back in California.*

The door handle clicked as I pushed it, and the big wooden door opened. The aroma from the antique wood brought up emotion up in me that was familiar yet uncomfortable. I couldn't put my finger on it, but wood smells evoked deep emotions of sadness within me.

The first room I walked through was full of paperwork and empty of people. I didn't see anyone around until I looked in the back of the next room. Two people were sitting in a room, dimly lit and full of shadows, leaving them silhouetted, but I was able to see it was a man and a woman.

"We're here, ma'am. Come on back to us." I recognized the woman's voice as the same voice from the outside speaker.

Walking toward the voices, I said, "Okay, hi. I'm Abigail. Abigail Blue."

"Hi, Abigail. We are getting ready to leave for the day but how can we help ya?" asked the man as he leaned forward and came out of the shadow. I saw his face and recognized it immediately. Memories flooded back as I studied his face. He had interviewed me several times, prepping me for the trial, and he had told me that I'd have to say uncomfortable words. Flashing back, I saw myself in the witness chair, and I could recall my mouth being wet and slimy on the microphone as I said the exact words he told me to say: *vagina and penis and anus.* I also smelled the wood aroma of the old courtroom.

The microphone echoed my shaky voice, and there were many people in the courtroom that day. They stared while I fumbled through my nightmare loudly. They were the witnesses to my nightmare, the nightmare of not being believed. I was the guilty one to them.

"W-well," I stammered, "I'm not sure where to start. I'm sorry I didn't call. I was walking through town and on the phone with Leroy Roth and sort of stumbled on your office. Leroy said it was okay to ring the bell. I'm here in town, finally dealing with my past. I was a client of yours in nineteen eighty-one. I was a rape victim, and you were my lawyer. I don't have much memory of what happened in court, and I don't know where to start or what to ask you because I wasn't planning on this. Wow, I'm rambling. I am nervous and I don't know what to say. I'm sorry."

His expression was one of concern, not judgment. "Abigail Blue? That's familiar. Nineteen eighty-one was such a long time ago. Why now, Abigail?" Mr. Lovell asked.

"Because, Mr. Lovell, along with my virginity, they stole my voice." Tears trickled down my cheek. "It's been thirty years, and I'm just now brave enough to come do this. I've been too afraid to come back to town and too embarrassed even to say my name aloud. I was the town slut when I left here. I'm not proud that it's taken so long, but I am compelled to now know more. I do not remember much. What I'd love to know is *whatever* you can tell me. I have no particular questions." I wiped my tears away, trying to look strong.

Mr. Lovell was also wiping away tears. "I remember your case now. I don't remember a lot of the details because it's been so long and I'm old now, ya know?" he joked, but I could tell he was also serious. "What I remember is that injustice took place. Those boys did you wrong, and they got away with it. The courts failed you, and I failed you. I'm so sorry." More tears fell from his eyes, and the compassion I felt for him seemed a little backward but strong nonetheless. My softening feelings compelled me to take a step toward him, but I stopped. I stood firmly on my own ground, not really knowing what was appropriate.

Yet I thought, *He isn't my enemy. What would it be like to work in the justice system and witness the heartbreak of innocent victims losing in the court of law?* Here he was, now a judge, no longer a state-assigned prosecutor. He had surely had years and years of experience with many heartbreaking cases like mine.

We stood still, looking at each other. My heart broke with his, and time stood still for a brief moment as we both mourned the injustice without saying anything.

"Abigail, I'm very sorry for failing you," he said silently, looking down.

"Mr. Lovell, I don't know why God allowed this to happen, but He did and I do trust Him. I am okay—I really am. Throughout the years and on my journey, He has given me strength and trust in Him. I will be okay if I don't get the answers I'm looking for; it would just be nice to know more, to fill in the black holes of my memory. One of the hardest things about this is the memory loss of my own past, but if I don't get it, I'll still be okay."

"You are a strong survivor, Abigail. I hate to cut you off, but we have to get to our granddaughter's birthday party. You are going to help so many others who don't know how to be free within the injustice of the system. Please find your voice, for it's a beautiful one. When you are ready to write the book that I think is in you, you come on back and interview me. I'd love to help out." His voice was thick with emotion.

*Write the book.* There it was again. How did he know there was a book simmering from within.

"Okay, I'll do that. Thank you so much for your time, and enjoy the party." I hugged him, silently promising myself to plan my next trip back as soon as possible and making a mental note to e-mail him as soon as I got to my computer so that we could stay in touch. It took me too long to get to him—thirty years—and I wasn't about to lose this connection!

The next day, on the flight out and exhausted, I flopped

into the seat, hoping to doze off for most of the flight. I leaned my head on the window; the coolness felt rejuvenating to my skin. As we accelerated into the air, I gave a deep sigh of relief. As I thought back on the past several days, I wanted to pat myself on the back. I had done a good job. This was not something I was used to saying to myself, but I really did feel good with the outcome of this trip.

Reconnecting with myself was huge, and as we flew up over the clouds, I truly felt I could float on them. Content with my unexpected outcome, I realized how wide-awake I really was. With no sleep in sight, I pulled out my Bible study on the Promised Land and figured I would finish it up. I was completely disinterested, but I knew I could whip through the last week's assignment in a couple of hours so that at least on the last day of being with my group, I'd appear to be caught up.

That didn't happen. I sat in utter awe as I read only the first paragraphs.

"In our session eight video, we circled around the children of Israel in a place of profound significance. Gilgal was their first stop in the Promised Land, just west of the Jordan River. There they set up twelve stones of remembrance and bore the mark of God's covenant by observing the rite of circumcision. No longer could they be called an unbelieving generation. When the nation of Israel reached Gilgal, a name meaning *circle*, they had indeed come full circle. God removed their shame, and they could finally put Egypt behind them.

"In some dimension, a Gilgal exists for any child of God who is willing to follow Him there by faith. Consider our Gilgals the places where we realize that God has rolled away our shame, proved us victorious in a do-over (an opportunity to go back and get something right), or taken us full circle in a significant way."

*Circle* took on a whole new meaning, and I fell in love with the word *Gilgal.* I wanted to shout out to my fellow passengers, "Can you see Him? Can anyone see Him? He's right here with me!"

*How can He be this intimate with me? Me, the unworthy and terrified girl. Me! He has chosen me to do circles with Him, to heal!*

A root of faith grew deep, despite being thirty thousand feet in the air at that moment. How could God be so big and expect my feeble mind to understand the mystery of all that was happening? It was all so much bigger than I was.

Closing the study book, I stared out the window for a long time and allowed the peace to grow. I decided that I wanted my Promise Land. I didn't know what it would look like, but I knew I wanted to be in it.

I felt full circle and completely content. I was ready to move forward in my life and shut the door on the past. What I didn't realize was that in shutting that door to the past at that point, I inadvertently created a root of settling for mediocrity. I didn't persist to find more truth then. I didn't write then. All *this* seemed so amazing and big, and I was content with where I was, yet there was so much more to come and I almost missed it.

# Chapter 6

# *Oneness*

Just a few short months ago, before shutting the door to my past, Matt and I had had our first date on the beach. We'd walked, talked, and laughed. Our hands accidentally brushed each other's as we walked along the coastline in San Diego, California.

We talked about our lives, our families, our misfortunes, our accomplishments, and ourselves. We talked as if it were our one hundredth date. We laughed so much. We both have a good sense of humor, and it was just plain fun to get to know the details of this man with whom my soul had instantly connected.

About halfway through our walk, we came across a group of seagulls sitting at the water's edge. They were sitting very still and seemingly concentrated on something.

Matt said, "I believe they're worshiping God." He proceeded to tell me the story running through his beautiful mind. He told me how Sam, one of the seagulls (I've now learned that he names most animals), was probably thanking his Maker for the food he had received today. Sam was probably thanking his papa for the wind blowing through his handsome feathers, and Lucy was probably thanking

God for Sam—her flying partner. "They have to know that He is their source. It has to be such a natural conversation between bird and God, don't you think?"

I fell in love that very moment.

Being back home was confusing. I had been sharing every detail with my new friend, and now that connection was gone. I had not let too many people in on what I was doing in Kentucky, so I didn't have anyone to reach out to. Sitting down at the computer, I connected the only way that was left for us. E-mail.

> *Dear Matt,*
>
> *Having gone through so much in Kentucky and returning home this time without being able to share it with you is difficult. I thought you were a part of my journey. I don't know what happened and why you are not talking with me anymore. It's confusing. I miss your smile, and I miss your understanding nods when I talk. I miss being listened to. Maybe I just needed to do this alone and this is exactly what was supposed to happen, except, well, it just hurts to wonder if I shared too much with you and that maybe the very thing that I loved about you, your connection to my story, well, maybe I was wrong. Maybe it's all too much for you. If so, I'm truly sorry.*
>
> *Thank you for being there for me while you were.*
>
> *I wish you the best,*
>
> *Abigail*

It didn't take long for him to respond, and I was elated to hear that he was *scared* and that he too felt strong feelings, as I did, and that he didn't know what to do with those feelings. He got scared and ran. While I was gone, he realized that he wanted me in his life.

We dated for nine months, and then we got married. Almost immediately, the drug relapses started, beginning the battle of destruction versus forgiveness. My focus was instantly turned to my current circumstances, and the book, my story, my voice—all of it—got put on hold once again. I was silenced again, first by overwhelming happiness, then by one overwhelming trauma after another.

Before we married, we prayed. We counseled and then we prayed some more. Most people felt we were rushing into things, but I knew in my spirit that he was the man I wanted to go through life with. I knew that meant dealing with the issues both of us had from our pasts. I brought a past with a lot of neglect and abuse. He brought a past with a lot of addiction and a heavy heart from several hidden and unresolved traumas in his own life.

We both felt the power of the Lord had healed us *enough* to get married. Again, we counseled and prayed and certainly didn't expect to have been completely whole before getting married. We believed that for us, marriage was God's way of continuing the healing in us. We talked about getting through life's toughness together. We talked about not just loving each other during the good times, but loving each other even *more* when life wasn't going to be easy. We promised each other this on our wedding day.

My son gave me the honor of walking me down the aisle, and our friend Jill sang "The More I Seek You" and "How Great Is Our God" during our ceremony. The idea of singing "How Great Is Our God" was to show our friends and family that it was God who had and who would continue to be glorified through our oneness.

We danced. We toasted. We ate cake, threw the bouquet, and off we went on our honeymoon.

Our one-month wedding anniversary is when the first hit to our marriage happened. Matt's past addiction reared its ugly head, and I felt betrayed when I found out he had relapsed on drugs and had been texting with other women. He said they were just friends and that I didn't have anything to worry about. I pushed away the gut feelings.

Devastated by this, I still managed to stand by him because he said it would never happen again and because I promised God that I would. God said He would be with me and He would bring hope and healing. He told me to stand firm on this promise.

Also, I was silenced. I was too concerned of what *they* would think if our marriage ended after only one month. Over time, and desperate to show everyone (or perhaps just myself) that we had a good, solid, happy marriage, I tolerated one relapse after another.

It's amazing how quickly two years flies by when you are turning a blind eye.

When we received the invitation to Pop's ninetieth birthday party, I relaxed and committed to enjoying the celebration without flaw. I didn't want anything to do with digging up the past. I simply wanted to celebrate my grandfather's ninety years of a good life with my family.

My prayer was, "God, please let me enjoy this time. Please allow me a bit of normalcy. God, if You want me to deal with anything while I'm back in town, You'll have to bring it to me and make it obvious."

One thing I've learned since is that God takes our prayers very seriously!

# Chapter 7

# Apology's Power

## Little Mountain, 2011

Standing at the check-in table where I was working, I watched him from afar. Holding onto his cane, he walked across the room toward his place at the head of the table. At ninety years old, his movements were still rather slick. What an accomplishment! My grandfather was amazing.

As he scooted into the chair at the head table, I saw him scanning the room, taking in all of his friends and family who were there with him this special day. He was not a man of much emotion, and yet today I could see an unfamiliar look on his face. *Is he feeling pain?* Nilda turned to him and whispered something in his ear. He patted her hand with his, reassuring her, and me from afar that he was fine. If he was not in pain, was he looking for someone?

I turned back to the task at hand, manning the sign-in table. A man and a woman approached, and I wondered if I knew them. As they filled in their names on the tags, I realized I definitely didn't know them. *Were they cousins? On whose side? Should I know them and I'm just forgetting?*

Looking around the room I felt like a stranger. *Who are these people? These people are my family, aren't they?*

Leaving this town years ago meant leaving this family. Missing out on knowing my own family hurt deeply. I should recognize these faces and know about them. I should be all up in their business and they in mine. Knowing my family was added to my list of things stolen. The anger began boiling inside, and I didn't realize that I was in a daze until the man called Billy Ray said, "Hey, aint' ya saposed to take our picture?"

"Oh, I'm sorry. I got lost in my thoughts, Billy Ray!" I grabbed my camera and directed them toward the backdrop. "Just step right over here and I'll take your picture for you!"

After I photographed the couple, signed in a few more groups of strangers—I mean *family*—and snapped their pictures, I took a few deep breaths in and realized that I was happy that this trip was all about getting reacquainted with them. It felt good to not be researching and trying to find "the boys." I was glad I'd surrendered this trip to God!

A few more deep breaths in, feeling rejuvenated and joyful, I turned to help the next guest who was standing at the table.

"Hi there. Just go ahead and sign in, and when you're done, I'll take your photograph for the Facebook online family album we're creating," I said to the man.

"Oh, I'm not here as a family guest. My name is Abel Broderick, the principal of the local high school, and I am here to present the birthday boy with this award." He pointed to the folder he was holding.

His last name struck a chord with me, one of anxiety and fear, and I stared blankly at him. He continued speaking. "I won't have much time today, as I have another appointment. I'm sorry. I wish I didn't have to make things difficult by rushing out. It looks as if you are going to have a great party here today."

I continued staring at him.

*Broderick. Abel Broderick.* It rang repeatedly in my head. I had been searching for information on my rapists for years, and here before me now stood one of Graham's brothers, Abel.

I looked him in the eyes and realized that he looked like an older version of his brother. He had the same blond hair and the same blue eyes. I had to remind myself that he wasn't Graham … However, he was the closest to him I'd ever gotten.

From the shock, I didn't introduce myself. I didn't even appear to be listening to what he was saying.

"Are you related to Graham?" I finally blurted out.

He stopped, and it was his turn to look at me with a blank look on his face.

"No. Why? Which one?" He stumbled with his words.

"Graham. Broderick," I said confidently. I knew he was his brother.

He looked at me intently. "This can't be good. Yes, Graham is my brother. This just can't be good."

"It's … well … It's different," was all I could manage to say to him.

We stood there sharing blank expressions, both in some sort of agreed-upon silence where neither of us knew what to say.

"So when you are done giving this award, can we go outside and talk for a moment?" I asked him.

Just then, Uncle Hank, my grandfather's namesake, spoke into the microphone. "Welcome, everyone. My name is Hank, Jr., Hank Deckert's youngest son. I want to welcome all of our family and friends to this special event celebrating my father's milestone birthday of ninety years! Could I ask you all to take a seat and let's get this party started!"

"This just can't be good," was all Abel could muster as he walked away.

I hoped that meant he was willing to talk to me.

*How on earth am I going to focus on anything other than this man?* He was sitting in front of everyone but off to the side of the head table. Occasionally he glanced at me with inquisitive looks, probably wondering who in the world I was.

The presentations began with Brother Bob. He was the local preacher and he had known Pop for years. He started with prayer, and an intense feeling of warmth started from my head and slowly drifted through my entire body, ending with my toes. Immediate peace engulfed me.

"Hank Deckert wears many hats," Brother Bob stated. From a box he had on the table, the preacher brought out several hats and had us all busting up with laughter within minutes. He told stories of how Pop wore a farmer's hat, a military hat, a sensitive hat, a "what was that?" hat. Each hat that was brought out had a significant story that told of the honor and grace of my grandfather.

When Brother Bob finished, he hugged Pop and told him how much he loved him. I saw that look in my grandfather's eyes again. What was it? I'd never seen it before.

Uncle Hank spoke next and began telling a story about his youth as Pop's son. The story included my grandmother, and when I looked at my Pop, I saw him wiping his eyes. His head was lowered, and he was crying! I'd never seen him cry.

In that moment, I realized how much he truly missed Grandma, his first wife. He had lived ninety years, the last fifteen without her. Grandma and Pop had known Nilda and her husband for many years. At the time Grandma died, Nilda had also recently lost her husband of many years.

Pop and Nilda became companions and married in order to have a friend at all times. It was a sweet friendship, but they were not soul mates. When they married, they talked with us, the family, about how they wanted to be buried next to their deceased spouses, but they wanted to live the rest of their lives together, as companions, and for several years, that is exactly what they had done.

All these years, especially with the miles between us, it had escaped me that Pop was with Nilda but missing Grandma. I wanted to run up and hug him. I wanted to take him in my arms and tell him it was going to be *okay*. But I also knew that it was good for him to cry.

The sweet moment was interrupted as Uncle Hank introduced Abel Broderick and he presented the award to Pop. Turns out, it wasn't an award; he presented Pop with his high school diploma. The original had apparently been lost many years ago, and my aunt thought it would be nice to replace it.

I thought it was kind of random. With so many things missing from our family, so many emotions got pushed to the side, yet diplomas and awards were important. I didn't understand why it was important to my grandfather, but I celebrated as I clapped, giving him the recognition of so much more than a high school achievement.

He had fought in World War II and raised four children in a stable home. He kept my grandma laughing her whole life. These feats were no small thing. Perhaps this diploma was symbolic of graduating from this life. He had accomplished so much, and he deserved the recognition.

Looking around the room, I wondered how many ways this man had affected each person. My mom sat in her wheelchair, chin held high in obvious honor and regard for her daddy. Aunt Maggie's smile clearly demonstrated her happiness with her father. Uncle Hank stood proudly to the side, happy and full of respect for his father and mentor.

Abel shook hands with everyone, gave Pop a hug, and then started walking toward the door. Jumping from my seat, I walked beside him.

"Can we talk for a minute? I know you're in a hurry, but it would mean so much to me for a minute of your time," I said.

He opened the door for me, motioning me before him. "So … what is this about?" he asked reluctantly.

"Do you remember the rape case that your brother was involved in?"

"Yes. I do."

"Well, that was me." I was amazed at the confidence I felt. My voice was not shaking, but a shift in my soul, of who I was, had taken place.

"What? Wow … I don't know what to say." His voice sounded a bit shaky as he continued. "I am so sorry."

In that moment, I didn't even realize the impact of his words. I was more concerned with the time since he had made it clear he only had a few minutes.

"I have had one question for many years," I said, feeling confident and strong as I looked right into his eyes. "Did he ever rape again? He got away with it with me; did he repeat it?"

He couldn't look at me, his head hung low, but he said, "Graham has been in a lot of trouble his whole life. I am just so sorry. I don't know what to say to you."

"I don't need you to say anything … I don't know what to ask, really … It's just always been something that's felt so undone for me."

Shifting his eyes from the ground to my face, he looked me squarely in the eyes. "I want you to know that I was in college when that happened. I didn't come back here to Little Mountain until after he was told to leave town. He has been disowned by our family, brought back in, disowned again … He comes and goes. He does well, then screws up and is not heard from for quite some time. We hope the silence means he is doing okay, but we just never know. I will tell you that he lost a child. She died on the operating table." His eyes seemed a bit confused, matching my heart.

Out of the corner of my eye, I could see my uncle staring out the windowed door toward us, probably wondering what was going on. I knew he would wonder why I was outside talking with this stranger while the family was inside celebrating my grandfather's birthday. I knew he was going to come check on me. I knew our time together was over.

"Abel, thank you for taking the time to talk with me. It means a lot," I said. I wanted a few more minutes with him just because it had been a long journey to get to this moment. At the same time, I didn't like the compassion that welled up inside me when he told me about the death of Graham's child. I wouldn't wish the death of a child on my own worst enemy.

I felt so small.

Abel turned, looked at me, and said, "Again, I'm so sorry and don't know what else to say."

"You don't owe me an apology, Abel. It's not your faul—"

He quickly interrupted me. "Yes, I do. Someone does."

I heard the words this time. "Thank you." My knees went weak, and a wave of dizziness came over me. Three little words—*I'm so sorry*—undid me. Even though it wasn't Abel's responsibility, I suppose I did need to hear them.

In that moment if felt as though I may have needed the acknowledgment more than the answers.

As Abel walked away, I turned to go back inside to Pop's party. There stood Uncle Hank, holding the door for me. As I walked through the open door, I allowed the words of apology to penetrate, fueling me on to continue my journey, and the next day I shocked myself by going where I went.

~An Author First~

The odor from the old wood walls overwhelmed me as I opened the courthouse main door and entered the long hallway. My heart dropped into my stomach.

*I can't believe I'm actually doing this.*

After talking with Abel at the party, I knew I needed to set aside my desire to *not* investigate while I was here. I knew I needed to take advantage of my time in town, so I decided to try to get the court transcripts in person.

On the walls were photographs of Old Little Mountain. There was a photograph of the courthouse from the 1800s. The town didn't look much different.

To my right was an empty courtroom. The door was partially open. As I walked past it, I could feel the despair from being in a similar courtroom three decades ago. I believe that our courtroom was upstairs, but for all I remember, it could have been this very room. I was too young, and the memories were pushed too far down for me to really know for sure. I do know that the thirteen-year-old girl in me could feel it. It was as if my mind didn't have the memory but my body was able to know exactly what had taken place and where. I shuddered as the fear took over, owning me in that moment.

*I wanted to puke.*

"Howdy." The clerk smiled. Her name tag said Laura. She asked me what she could do to help me. I told her that I was there for old court transcripts from a case I was involved in many years ago.

"Okay," she said, her Southern drawl evident. Then she asked the question I'd been dreading. "What are the names of the persons involved in the case?"

The day had come. I had to say the names aloud. I had to say it while standing in this town. For all I knew, Laura could have been his cousin. It's likely that if she wasn't, her boss was. That's how it is in small towns.

I stated the facts. "My name is Abigail Blue, the defendant's name was Graham Broderick, and the case took place in April of 1981."

As she wrote our names down on her paper, things shifted from *sur*real to *very* real.

"What was the nature of the case?" Laura asked.

"Rape. I was the victim in the case, and I'm here to try to retrieve the court transcripts."

As my mouth was moving and the words were coming out, my mind was having its own conversation, or I should say argument, with itself.

*Do I tell her why I need these records?*

*She'll think I'm nuts.*

*I shouldn't be here.*

*Yes, I should.*

*I deserve answers.*

*These people are going to think I'm nuts.*

Laura looked at me, her head cocked to the side, and interrupted my personal conversation by asking, "Were the parties involved minors or adults?"

"I was thirteen, and he was nineteen," I stated as her head shifted to the right.

She looked confused.

"Laura, I live in California, and I've been trying for years to retrieve these records through the mail. The paperwork I did receive is not the transcript from court, just the administrative paperwork. There are subpoenas and other admin stuff, but no transcripts."

She asked if the judgment was included in the paperwork I had received. I told her the truth.

"There was no judgment. It was a 'not guilty' verdict."

"Oh, didn't you say you were a minor?" she asked.

"Yes, I did."

As Laura disappeared to go find my long-awaited information, my mind wandered. I'm not sure where it went, exactly. I suppose it was headed to the same location it's been every time I even think about unburying these records: *nowhere*. Just the same dead end.

When the fear and anxiety well up, I usually zone out or find something else to think about. But here I was at the courthouse, actually doing something about it. My mind couldn't wander, and I couldn't find something else to do. The fear was so big and ferocious that it was unavoidable. I broke out in a sweat and thought my heart was going to jump out of my chest. I was close to having to sit down for fear of collapsing.

I still wanted to puke.

Instead, I whispered a prayer. "God, do something big here." As I prayed, I felt a strange assurance and knew that God would answer. I just couldn't envision *how*. What on earth could ease this crazy big fear?

Leaning on the counter for balance, I took several deep breaths in and was shocked by how loud and strong my heart was beating. *What am I afraid of anyway? I'm an adult and I'm safe, aren't I?* I tried to convince myself that no one was going to hurt me.

I heard someone move behind me, and I turned to see a mother and her five- or six-year-old son walk in. I wondered if I "knew" her and if I was going to have to say my name again. *Will she recognize me? Is she one of them? I wonder if I'd even recognize the girlfriends of the boys from that night. I mean, it's been so long.*

I still wanted to puke. I needed strength.

Then …

The little boy started singing. "Jesus loves me. This I know, for the Bible tells me so. Little ones to Him belong; they are weak but He is strong … Yeeeeeees, Jesus loves me … Yeeeeesss, Jesus loves me …"

The desire to fall on my knees and sit at Jesus's feet right there in the court's admin office was overwhelmingly strong. The little boy's voice gave me courage. I could feel it rising up as he continued singing behind me.

Laura interrupted my ruminations. "I'm having a hard time finding the files," she said, staring at me.

"Look, I know this was a long time ago. I need you to know something; I'm not here to cause trouble. My request isn't meant to drudge up information on him." I pointed my finger to his name on the paper where she had written everything. "It's not even really about me." I pointed my finger to my name on the paper. This is about the injustice done over three decades ago. I'm doing research for a book I'm writing. I'm speaking up about the injustice that was done to me. I'm finding my voice. But, Laura, I want help in remembering things and how they happened. That is all. I'm *not* here to cause trouble. This is a *God* thing and I hope you can understand what I'm saying."

Quietly I hoped she was one of the Bible Belters; otherwise, bringing God into this was not going to help my case!

Laura turned away without saying a word, leaving me feeling dumbfounded at what I'd just said. *That was a lot to tell a stranger!*

I saw her go over to someone else's desk, and I heard her say, "There is an author here. She wants information on this case for research. She was the victim in the case." I barely heard anything else.

*She called me an author.*

*She didn't call me the rape victim first.*

She returned to the counter, and I took the Post-it note that she handed me as she matter-of-factly said, "Here. This is the best I could do. I doubt it will get you very far, but it's the only chance of your getting the transcript. This is the phone number for the court reporter on your case. I wish you the best."

I thanked her numerous times before I turned and ran to my car. I didn't remember the hallway, and I didn't notice the smell of the old wood as I ran out of the courthouse.

*The court reporter's phone number—are you kidding me!*

My hands were shaking so much that I had to dial three different times.

The phone rang, and rang, and rang.

Finally, a woman answered. "Hellooooo." She sounded so sweet and *Southern*.

"Hi, this is going to be a very strange request, but my name is Abigail, and I just got your name from the Harlan County Courthouse. I'm looking for a court transcript that you reported on in 1981. It's a very important case to me … I'm the vict—"

"I will just interrupt you right now." Her voice was no

longer so sweet, now laced with irritation. "I shredded all my files seven years ago. I do not have any legal files here at my house. I was only required to hold them for ten years, and I held all the files for much longer than required. I'm sorry, but I'm not going to be able to help you—not at all."

There wasn't much for me to say. She had shut me out before I could even think of what else to ask. "Well, is there *any* other way? I begged, the desperation embarrassing.

"No, ma'am. I'm sorry I can't help you, and I have to go now." She hung up and that was that. I knew I was never going to get my hands on the records. They were simply gone—permanently, just like the jury members, a dead end. I did the only thing left to do at this point. I sobbed. I sat in my car in front of the bank on Main Street, and sobbed until snot ran from my nose and dripped onto my lap.

The grief was overwhelming—the death of hope, the hope to recover a lifetime of questions and loss.

Letting go was becoming the theme to this story of mine, the unanswered questions an injustice all their own.

Eventually, I opened my eyes and took in the scene. Here I was on Main Street in Little Mountain. I'd walked to this bank with my grandmother so many times as a child. F & H Drug Store stared at me from across the street. Cherry Cokes and french fry memories lived there. I hadn't been in that store in over thirty years, and I could still smell the combination of the frying grease mixed with the cleanliness of the pharmacy, the aroma always slapping me in the face when I'd go pick up Grandma's prescriptions. Oh, how I loved it! Grandma had always slipped me a quarter before I left so I could get my Cherry Coke treat.

I almost got out of my car to go get that savored Cherry Coke, but I wouldn't allow myself that luxury. Instead, I put the car in gear and headed back to Mom's.

The twenty miles to Alba helped balance my emotions. I sang as loud as I could, pouring it all out within the confines of my car. With each angry belt of a lyric, I let go. Or perhaps it was more like I *threw it away*. I didn't want to be a part of any of this frustrating journey anymore. Twenty miles didn't seem near long enough.

As I drove past Jeston Lovell's office, I thought I should stop in to interview him. After all, he told me I could, but I was too angry. No more getting my hopes up high, only to be let down with unanswered questions. So I kept driving. As I got past the center of town, I knew deep down that I wouldn't be seeing him again. *Am I going to be okay if I never get the transcripts or the answers? And what is the question anymore, anyway?*

Confused, I just kept driving. It was all too much for one day—all too much for one lifetime.

It was easy to set it all aside for the remainder of the trip. We had an uneventful and relaxing few days as we enjoyed visits with family. We spent the majority of our time with Mom in the nursing home, making small talk and worrying about the weather. Going back home to California was another story. As much as I wanted to continuing escaping, that would no longer be an option.

The bright light from truth was about to invade my life.

# Chapter 8

# *Mama Moments*

San Diego, California, 2012

Footings and foundations are to homes what feet and legs are to the human body: footings anchor the home to the ground and support the foundation, which in turn carries the weight of the home.

One thing that is so heartbreaking about living with an addict is that he loses the beautiful parts of his mind while he is out there living for his drug. Nothing in and around the world matters, except that dark, ugly drug. Nothing, and I mean *nothing*, else matters. Jobs are lost, wives are abandoned, medical issues are ignored, and painful consequences are birthed.

The addict goes out on a "run" and the wait begins. The wait begins for him to come to his senses. You wait and wonder if he understands that your whole life has just been pulled out from under you like a slippery rug. You wonder if he understands that you have to do what's best for yourself, because he isn't. You have to protect yourself and yet still love the addict, and you wonder if he still loves you.

*Does he still hear God?*

*How long will it take for him to choose differently?*

As the wife of a drug addict, huge decisions have to be made: decisions first as a mother. Even though my children are adults, they still observe and watch and learn. As a business owner, I've had to make some big decisions that I never wanted to make, all without the help of the man who has been connected to my soul ever since we met.

*Do I remove all the vehicles so that he doesn't drive drunk and kill someone? Do I empty out the bank account so that I'm not left in debt or broke? Do I leave the house or does he? If I decide he is the one to leave, do I legally remove him if he refuses to go? If I decide he is the one to leave, am I safe? Or do scary people now know where I live? How do I tell my children that he is causing chaos and is completely out of his mind again? Do I tell them these things? Do I keep the business afloat? If so, how do I do that when he is the tradesman doing all the day-to-day work? Do I hire permanent employees or just temporary, until he returns to a place of sanity again?*

*Do I end it all and divorce this man or do I love him unconditionally and stay? If so, how do I do that and protect myself at the same time?*

I decided to temporarily move out of the house and leave him to his own choices. This meant couch hopping for me. My friends each took a turn and allowed me to stay with them. Sometimes I got my own room by way of a empty guest room. It was a gift when that happened because I could safely let the tears flow.

Being away from my own house meant that I had no idea what was happening there. I had to learn to let go, tune in, and hear from God. I remember one day asking Him to give me an internal stoplight. I needed God to give me a green light when He wanted me to go, a yellow for when I needed to pause, and a red for the times when I needed to simply stop and not make any moves forward. Those were the hardest, but I did manage to find peace in the midst of the recurring storms.

The journey to peace in the midst of this was not a fast one, nor was it an easy one. When you know the rug is being ripped out from underneath you, you cry out and ask for it not to be. You beg for something different to take place. You try to stop the train that is speeding toward you, and then you realize you don't have the power to do that, so you simply get out of the way.

As I walked on the beach one day, accepting my place (out of the way), I surrendered to the reality that big changes would be taking place. I was considering a legal separation, and I had to fire my own husband from our business. I could only hope these actions could be reversible. The weight of our home fell on me.

But God tells me that I am to affirm my trust in Him and to wait hopefully in His presence. *And then I'm to watch to see what He'll do.*

Still, change scares me.

Walking along the beach, lost in thought, I looked up and saw a group of seagulls, reminding me of the day I fell so head over heels in love with my husband. I remembered him talking with me about how Sam and Lucy, the two seagulls on our first date, talked with God.

I remembered my husband's heart and how normal it—*he*—seemed then. How normal and natural it felt to be with him. That day on the beach with him, I had no idea of the *ab*normalcy and insanity that was about to break into my life. Maybe that day on the beach was just that, a walk on the beach, not the fairy-tale-knight-in-shining-armor happy ending I had hoped for.

In the three years of our marriage, the "normalcy" we created hadn't been all that normal. Relapses occurred about every six months, and it was never a small deal. We usually ended up physically separated and financially broke by the time it was all over. Matt's relapses usually started with popping a pill to feel better, "just once," and generally ended with a crack pipe and his consumption of gallons of alcohol. He either ended up in jail or sober living facility, and I was left with the mess of cleaning up the house. The vicious cycle left me feeling overwhelmed and confused.

Instead of focusing on the amazing story unfolding in Little Mountain, over the past couple of years, my mind began to pay attention only to the circumstances in front of me. Being wrapped up in the unfolding disaster of drug addiction, I got stuck in the darkness, with joy slowly dissipating from my life.

My walk on the beach was done. The sun had set, and the seagulls had all flown off to wherever they go when it's dark.

Throughout the weeks that followed, light found its way into the darkness, and in that illumination, I was able to see my own addictions and strongholds come out of the shadows. I thought that getting out of the way was for Matt to see his darkness; instead, I came face-to-face with my own demons, lurking always in the shadows. It was exhausting, but I couldn't help but see the glaring patterns of codependency wrapped in and around the relationships throughout my life.

There wasn't any one situation that brought this revelation to me. It wasn't any one thing that someone said. I simply woke up the morning after my beach walk, when I watched the seagulls fly away, and I knew something was different.

As the light opened my eyes, I could never have imagined how my life would be changing for the good. Not in that dreadful dark moment of depression would I have ever have imagined such a deep healing was about to take place.

I woke up that morning and went to church as I usually did, except attending church without Matt was depressing and embarrassing. Like the other regulars in our church, we had our own spot in the church. It was always so obvious when he was relapsed. Instead of attending church in neatly kept clothes and my normal put-together self, I'd show up wearing sweatpants, a baggy shirt, and greasy hair in a ponytail, my face red and eyes swollen from having cried all night. I always sat in our normal chairs on the right side, two aisles from the back. I suppose I was holding his seat.

I'd sit there and let the tears flow. They were somewhat uncontrollable anyway since there were so many that they couldn't be turned off, even if I had tried. But I didn't try; I just let them freely flow. The safety of my church environment allowed me to truly "come as I was."

Overwhelming tears were a part of my every day at this point. I mean, I'd been crying out to God for a while now, for my husband, for my marriage, for the little girl who was searching so desperately for a home to belong to.

But this day's cry was different. I sat there realizing that something so much bigger than all those things was missing. I was crying out for a mama. I was feeling the craving of a mother's love.

The nurturing love of my mother had been missing for many years. A few short months ago, I attended a healing retreat. At this retreat, we learned to heal, both physically and spiritually. But to receive the healing, one had to dig deep … and I dug up this desire, this need for nurturing love.

And then I buried it again.

My mind drifted, and I wondered what it would feel like to have the empty chair next to me filled by a mother's arms. I didn't even know how to imagine it. Imagining *giving* a hug was not hard; I could do that with my children. It was the receiving of the hug that I was so unfamiliar with.

Maybe the yearning had emerged because of the letters from Mom that I had read while back in Little Mountain. Maybe, just maybe, the little girl in me was reaching out, holding up her hands, and saying, "Please, Daddy, give me my mama."

It was shocking that I heard myself say it out loud.

Just then, a member of our church called on anyone suffering with depression to come up and receive prayer. As I listened to her talk, I fought with the idea of going up and receiving prayer. *I am not suicidal. I don't want to hurt myself. Yet my soul is so hurt and I am isolating ... Am I just around the corner from wanting just not to breathe?* I'd been there before, and I didn't want to go there again because it's a hard place to come back from.

Again, I was shocked with my outward response as I realized that I had gotten up and run to the woman speaking. I surrendered it all to God. I received prayer, and she asked God to fill my heart where it needed to be filled up.

As I turned and started walking up the aisle to leave church, feeling good about having reached out, there stood Winnie, a woman from my weekly home group.

We didn't really know each other. What we knew of each other was in passing and from hearing each other briefly speak at home group once a week, when I actually made it. My commitment wasn't that strong, so I rarely saw her.

Winnie opened her arms and offered me a hug. I accepted it ... her. She pulled me in close and something began. She started whispering to me. "It's okay, baby. Cry in my arms. It's safe to let it all out." So I did.

I sobbed and sobbed and sobbed. She nurtured my heart. I stayed in her arms, knowing God was giving me a "mama moment." In the quietness of my heart, I thanked Him. In those few moments, my heart was receiving something so deep, so rich, so nurturing. Years and years of a yearning heart were being ministered to.

I stood there holding on ... *I don't want to let this moment go.*

As if reading my mind, Winnie then said, "You need more of this. Come over this week so we can spend time together." The deep contentment from my soul was indescribable. An amazing, beautiful mama heard an unseen silent girl, and an amazing friendship began.

I accepted Winnie's offer and had lunch with her that next week.

That mama moment and first hug blossomed into a deep and very real bond. We have shared moments that I've never experienced with my own mother. She has done real life with me. Winnie has guided me, nurtured me, corrected me, accepted me, and some days she has just held me.

The hurts and injustices in life have kept my own mother at a distance from me. I know my mother loves me, and she knows I love her. Unfortunately, we haven't done life together, and that is what it takes to have the deep connection I have longed for all these years. I desperately want this with my own mother, and someday soon I hope to go and share it with her. I have to believe that as long as we are breathing, it's never too late.

My time with Winnie was a healing from the inside out, with a spotlight on the pattern of codependency in my own life. I could see how I had always been with an addicted partner to fill my own need to be a savior to someone.

Once I left my first husband, who, in hindsight, was not the nightmare I had thought he was at the time, I had jumped right into one relationship after another, each one ending because he couldn't be the savior that I needed.

Within all those relationships, I believed deep down that one man *could* save me, yet no man could love me deeply enough to touch the core of my being. They tried to love me in their best way possible, but even a healthy man (and there were a couple of healthy ones) couldn't make me happy and content. A mere human man couldn't calm the storm that needed to be silenced. The hole that lay inside my spirit was God-shaped—shaped perfectly so that no man could *ever* fill it.

What I expected from my men was an impossible task.

What I now know, in hindsight, is that just as God is the only One to fill the God-shaped hole in my soul, the foundation of my heart's home needed to be restructured. As much as I hated to admit it, Little Mountain was the foundation of my heart's home and there was work to be done there, a rebuilding.

Hearing from God is much different than I envisioned it to be. Before I knew how to hear from Him, I thought *those* people were nuts. God whispers to me, not with an audible voice, it's more of an impression or a very strong thought that I can't argue with. There is authority in it, and I always just know it's Him. When I don't like what He's saying, I question it's Him, but deep down, even then I know.

Many times I'll just be walking along, living my life, and I'll see something that stands out to me. I'll take a photograph, usually with just my cell phone, and later the image will come back to be extremely meaningful.

It can be trees leaning in on each other, and I will have it impressed upon me to *lean in for support.*

It can be the light shining on the road in just the right way, telling me that my *road is lit with precision.*

It can be walking to the right on the fork of an abandoned railroad track that tells me I am on the right track.

One day it was a heart-shaped rock in the midst of all the other ordinarily shaped rocks on the shore as I jogged along. As I went past it, I noticed its shape but kept going. I didn't get more than fifty feet away from it before I felt "nudged" to go back and find the heart amongst the rocks.

*Find the heart.*

Turning back, I searched for the rock until I found it. For the rest of the day, I couldn't get the saying out of my mind: *Find the heart.*

*Find the heart* was impressed upon me nonstop, all day.

"*Whose* heart, God?" I prayed, and as I did, I envisioned myself next to my mother's bed, writing.

"Am I to write my story sitting next to my mother, Lord?"

*No. That's not your story that you are writing.*

"Well, whose, then?"

*Find her heart, Abigail.*

Later in the evening, when I got the call that Pop was having major heart difficulties and was in the hospital, I knew I'd be going back to Little Mountain. After everything that had happened with Winnie, I knew it wasn't just his heart I'd be finding. It would be Mom's as well.

Nervously I planned yet another trip home to Little Mountain. As much as I yearned to be there for my Pop and to know my mother on a deeper level, I desperately wanted my husband to stay clean and involved in the recovery program he had recently committed to.

"You can trust me," Matt said when I approached him with the idea of my leaving again. "Not only can you trust me; I want to support you in this."

The morning I left, Matt prayed over my family and me. He prayed that we would be able to communicate our love for each other with a gesture and touch, no more empty words. He also prayed that it would begin from the first moment we saw each other. It was a beautiful prayer, and it gave me hope, not just for my current trip, but for our relationship as well.

*If only he could stay in this God-centered place ...*

# Chapter 9

# *Find the Heart*

Little Mountain, Kentucky, 2013

Once I got into town, I went straight to the hospital to see Pop. The doctors reassured me that he had had a minor setback throughout the night but he was now stable. He needed to rest, so visitors were being limited for the next two days. This allowed me time alone with Mom.

Matt's prayers of instant connection with my family were answered. The moment I stepped into my mother and stepdad's shared nursing home room, there was a strong sense of welcome and not the normal dread I had come to expect. Both she and my stepdad, Kennedy, were sitting up, she in her bed and he in his recliner chair. It was much different from the last time I had been here, when I was met with a sign on the door that said Do Not Disturb and I didn't see them until the late the next day.

When I walked in the room, we made instant eye contact and her eyes welled with tears as she smiled brightly. "Well, you finally made it! I've been sittin' here waitin' for ya, and ohhhh, I'm so happy you are here!" She giggled and motioned for me to come sit on her bed, next to her.

When I sat down, she reached for my hand and pulled it to her lap. She held on to it, *to me*, tightly. Instinctively, I responded by squeezing back and maintaining eye contact with her. "Well, thanks. I'm glad to be here!"

"How was your flight … and your drive?" she asked.

"Good and pretty uneventful," I responded.

"Daddy will be glad to see you, Abigail. You are a good granddaughter for coming all this way to see him, to care for him. It will mean so much to him." Her eyes welled up with tears once more. She was losing her father. We all knew it wouldn't be long before Pop would be leaving us. He was ninety-three years old, and with one medical condition after another, he had become very tired over the past year. He seemed ready. *Were we ready to let go?*

"Well, he is easy to love, ya know?" was all I could muster in return. "Do you want to go sit on the porch, Mom? Those rocking chairs looked pretty inviting as I came in …"

"Yes, let's go see if the cardinal is out there. He hangs out at the bird feeder sometimes, and we enjoy watching him bully the other smaller birds." She got up and into her wheelchair.

Kennedy chimed in. "I'll just let the two of youns' visit. I'm going to take a nap."

The rest of the afternoon was a comfortable time together, just Mom and me. We sat on the porch, watching and listening to the birds, thoroughly enjoying each other's company.

When I went to see her the next morning, I half-expected to be met with the Do Not Disturb sign on their door. My hopeless expectation was wrong as she was vibrant and cheerful, happy to see me.

"Good morning, Mom!" The excitement was evident in my tone.

"Well, hi! I'm so happy you're here. Come sit next to me on the bed," she lovingly invited. "Kennedy just left for his doctor's appointment, it's just you and me."

I barely fit on the side of her small bed, but then I leaned my arms on her legs. It was a bit awkward, but I didn't want to pull away.

"Abigail, grab me my ChapStick in my drawer right there," she said as she pointed to her nightstand. Opening the drawer, I saw a beautiful journal. Lifting it up, I found the ChapStick and handed it to her.

"This sure is a beautiful journal, Mom. Where did you get it?" I asked.

Images of soft pink and purple flowers filled the cover, with the words "Amazing Grace" written in the middle and bordered by lace. It was delicate looking.

"Oh yeah, that's been in there for a couple of weeks now. My counselor wanted me to write my story, and it's just been sitting in there 'cause I can't write anymore. My hands shake too much."

With tears welling up, I asked her, "Would you like me to write it for you, Mom?"

"Yes! Oh, yes! I would love that! I was hoping someone would want to help me out, and I'm so glad it's going to be you." She placed her hand on mine. Our eyes met, and no words on any paper could describe what it was like in that moment. It was as if both of us knew beforehand and were thanking God at the same time.

"Okay, then it's settled. I'll write it for you. When do you want to get started?" I asked.

"How about we have breakfast and then start?"

"Perfect. I just need you to know that my handwriting isn't going to be much better than yours!" I laughed.

"Well, that's hard to believe," she said as she gently pushed me off the side of the bed, scooting herself up; it was a gesture one would make toward someone she was familiar with. It felt nice.

After breakfast, we settled in and got started on her story. I curled up in the recliner that sat between her and my stepdad's hospital bed, and she positioned her bed to be sitting up. My mother began telling me her story, filling me in on some of the missing links to my own.

"I had a happy childhood, and the fact that we moved a lot with Daddy in the army wasn't a big stressor for us because we all had fun together and there wasn't anything in my childhood that I can really remember being negative.

"I was the second to the youngest, and Junior was the baby. I was his protector, and I would beat up anyone who messed with him. Until we got older, of course, and then he would protect me. I was close to all my siblings, the closest to Junior. Sissy and I did all the girl stuff, although she was much girlier than I was and she had a better sense of fashion, but we were close too. Logan and I had our own special kind of relationship because he was eight years older and we didn't really play together or anything when we were little. We became closer as we got to be adults, though.

"Our biggest adventure of the family was moving to Japan with the army. Mama had it hard to get us there because she met Daddy over there. The trip over was chaotic because we missed the bus and then the train too! I remember the airplane trip being really long and I slept a lot.

"Once we were in Japan, it wasn't as scary as I thought it would be, it was fun and exciting! We lived there for year and a half and then moved to New Jersey. That's where I met Terry." She looked up at me for a quick moment when she said his name, and I saw the flicker of joy. It was a quick moment that was gone too soon for me. I'd never heard her talk of loving my father.

She continued. "He went to high school with Sissy, and that is how we met. We courted and we married within a year. Shortly after that, Anne was born and I've never been so happy in all my life. She turned and looked toward her bulletin board with all her photographs on it and giggled as her eyes fell on the photo of Anne as a little girl.

We were very happy. Then we had you, and it was then that things took a turn for the worse. Terry had an affair, and it devastated me. But I was determined to make the marriage work.

"A couple years after you were born, we had another baby, but the baby didn't make it ... I gave birth to him as a stillborn. My baby boy was born dead, and I was depressed for months. I locked myself in a dark room. I've never in all my years felt that kind of pain."

The room fell silent, and my world stopped spinning. The raw silence was filled with truth and an understanding so powerful that it broke through the wall that had been erected so many decades ago.

I sat there in my seat knowing that familiar pain of a disloyal husband. I knew the pain of his addictions being stronger than the love for his wife. I knew the depth of that level of depression. I myself was barely making it out of that same pit. What I could not imagine was losing a child while buried in that horrible emotional pit.

I couldn't move the pen. I couldn't do anything at all. My eyes were frozen on the paper, and I could not look up into the eyes that I knew were focused in on me.

So many unrealized questions were answered. I never

really knew why we rarely touched or embraced. The wall kept intimacy out, and there was a broken bond between us, one much deeper than what the rape or distance had caused. It was something I'd always known but never allowed myself to accept.

Her gaze was heavy, but I wasn't ready to look up. Not yet. I knew with everything I had in me that I'd never be *ready* to hear whatever was next, maybe an apology, maybe an excuse for all the years of maintaining a superficial relationship. The wall held back the pain so well; the wall was just … easier. And it was holding back emotion I didn't feel capable of managing.

And, yet, it crashed so quietly.

Tears welled up and slid down my cheeks, the pain no longer imprisoned. I finally looked up and saw that I was right. She was gazing straight into my soul. Her eyes were soft and also had tears welling up in them.

She reached for my hand, and I received it. We had a mutual understanding of the pain, mixed with immediate forgiveness, freeing us both as we squeezed hands, seeing one another eye-to-eye, heart to heart.

"I've always loved you, Abigail. I'm sorry that I didn't know how to show it the way you've needed it."

Her words hit my heart in the same moment that I opened it up to her.

"Thank you, Mom. Living without you has been hard, and I know you love me."

It was a simple and sweet moment filled with so much power.

The transition into the rest of her story was natural as she shared how happy she was to be able to share a hospital room and live with my stepdad again.

Before he was admitted to the nursing home, she had

lived here without him, and the separation had made her anxious. But it was then that she met Flo, her roommate at the time. She talked about how happy her friend had made her feel. She talked about the other patients in the nursing home and how she enjoyed their company. She talked about her grandchildren with a smile.

She also talked about her death.

She shared how she was at peace and that she wasn't afraid. Somehow I was no longer afraid of what we had lost. I didn't like the loss of a lifetime together, but I was grateful for this day, this moment of healing.

The rest of the day was spent with my uncle joining us for a nice visit and we had a great family day. It may have been appeared very ordinary from the outside looking in. But, for me, it was simply extraordinary.

Later in the evening, I met with Jenny Hill, a friend from elementary school with whom I had reconnected on Facebook awhile back. She had written a book about her own journey of healing in losing her mother.

In her book, Jenny had described our hometown so beautifully, and she was able to share her pain and recovery in a compelling story. I wanted to reach out and ask her if we could meet the next time I was in town. Her quick response surprised me, and we quickly set up a time to meet while I'd be in town.

We met at McDonald's, where we sat and talked for hours. She listened as I told her my story. I didn't mention the paperwork or the jury list or anything in the present tense. I simply told her why I had left. She cried as she told me that she was so sorry and that she had no idea I had left for those reasons. Back then, it was understood around town that I had left to live with my dad in California and that no one really knew why I left so abruptly.

As she spoke, I quietly mourned for all the lost years.

Placing her hand on my arm, she asked, "What's wrong, Abigail? Are you okay?" I must have been so deep in thought that I had checked out.

"I'm s-sorry," I stammered. "The loss just overwhelms me. I don't even know what is real right now."

We sat in silence for a moment. Neither of us knew what to say or do.

"Can we pray, Abigail?" she asked.

We prayed out loud, right there in the middle of McDonald's, and we asked for peace and understanding beyond our own.

"God brought us together," she stated in a quiet voice. "My mom and your dad are in heaven, knowing the end of all this confusion."

Given that we both felt our parents' deaths had a lot to do with our own spiritual journeys, it wouldn't surprise me if she was right.

We continued talking, and I shared the jury list and the rest of the story with her. Explaining who was who evoked anxiety for me because she knew some of the people involved. When I told her who the defense attorney was, she shocked me by telling me that he went to my church.

"Wait. Calvin Cartway goes to my church?" I almost shouted. Even though it was his job as a defense attorney, the idea of facing the man who got the rapists' off was extremely intimidating.

"Yes, indeed he does," she stated.

Finally, the next day, I got the call that I could go see Pop. His eyes were dull, as though his light from within was dimming. *Was he in the last chapter of his life?* As we sat quietly in the hospital room, there was no need to fill the air with empty words. The acceptance of our individual struggle hung heavily in the air. He with his failing heart and mine feeling shattered to pieces with all the confusion and loss.

The doctor said he would be going home after a week's rest in the hospital. He would have to take it easy, and we both knew that the doctor's strict orders were necessary, but at the same time, it would be difficult for him since he was such a go-getter.

Sitting there holding his hand, we both stared out the window and simply waited together. It was refreshing not to talk, to feel comfortable enough just to *be*. I found a piece of Pop's heart in the silence, the piece that needed understanding and acceptance.

During that time, though, my mind wandered and I started to obsess about seeing Calvin Cartway. From my phone, I tried Googling his name to find a picture of him so that I could find him and talk with him on Sunday at church. I found nothing online about him. He was just another hidden clue I'd have to seek out.

Jenny had given me a brief description of him, but as I looked around in the church that next Sunday, it could have been 75 percent of the men there. It was painful. No one that matched his description was catching my eye when I looked at him, and I was terrified to go up and ask where I could find Mr. Cartway. I was a painful wreck by the time Sunday school was over and worship was about to begin. I had not comprehended a word from the lesson, and I knew that I wouldn't be able to enter into worship because of my anxiety.

I walked into the bathroom and quietly prayed in the privacy of the stall. I needed to focus on Jesus, my reason for loving the church so much. I was baptized there, and it was one of my favorite childhood memories. *God, if it's meant to be, bring him to me, if not, help me not think about it anymore.* I walked out of the bathroom and went to find a seat somewhere in the middle of the church. No longer would I be hidden in the back. I wanted to be seen.

And seen I was. As I went to sit down, two men in suits quickly approached me; the taller man reached out his hand to introduce himself to me, the newcomer. "Hi there!" he enthusiastically exclaimed. "I'm Calvin Cartway."

*What the ...?*

"Of course you are," I replied matter-of-factly, still shaking his hand.

*Lord, You are quick! I don't think I've ever had a prayer answered so quickly.*

The shorter man also reached out his hand to greet me, but I didn't hear him. He fell out of focus as my eyes zoned in on Mr. Cartway, who looked at me with a perplexed look on his face.

"I'm sorry. That was a crazy response. My name is Abigail Blue." I stood quietly as he stood still, put his hand on his chin, and looked at me, trying to figure it out.

*Was it my weird response to his greeting or did he recognize my name?*

It only took him about thirty seconds.

"Hmm ... You and I have had legal proceedings, haven't we?" he finally asked.

"Yes, sir. We sure have." I placed my hands on the side of the wooden pew to steady myself.

He kept looking at me, trying to remember who I was.

"It was a rape case in nineteen eighty-one, and I was the victim," I said, hoping to jog his memory.

Nodding his head in agreement, he said, "Yes, okay. Yes. Now I remember."

*Awwwwwkward.*

He continued. "Well, how are ya?" It was as if we had been on the same side of the case or something ...

111

*I am not playing this game with you, buddy.* "I am good, thank you. This is my first time in town. I mean, that's not true. I've been here before, but this is my first time showing myself in town. It's been over thirty years since I was able to do that. So, yeah, I'm finally good and it's finally good to be here."

*That felt good to say, but oh, he must think I'm crazy.*

"Well, it's good to have ya here today." He adjusted his tie, buttoned his suit jacket that was casually opened, and turned to walk away. "You have a good day now, ya hear?"

*Just like a good ole Southern boy to avoid it all.*

He went and sat down. His seat was five pews back, with a perfect view of me, but I couldn't see him. I turned and looked back to see him whispering to the woman sitting next to him.

As I sat down and turned around to face the front, the numbness hit and I could feel his eyes on my head. *What on earth is he telling his wife right now? Why did I have to sit here?*

Clasping my Bible tightly kept my hands from shaking. My heart was beating so fast and hard that I had a hard time believing the people around me couldn't hear it.

The music started, and I had to remember my prayer in the bathroom just ten minutes earlier. *Lord, I need you. I want to focus on You, Lord. Please help me do just that. Please calm my hands, Lord. And God, please don't let me cry.*

Two women walked up to the front and began strumming their banjos, and instantly my anxiety was relieved. Tears streamed down my face as they sang from their hearts, with mine joining in. I no longer cared who could see me.

*This would be my prayer, dear Lord, each day*
*You help me do the best I can*
*For I need Thy light to guide me day and night*
*Blessed Jesus, hold my hand*

As worship continued and the tears trickled down my cheeks, I felt acknowledged by God. I was in complete awe that that particular song would be played at that exact moment. Apparently, this was the day for quickly answered prayers.

The pastor came to the front during the end of the last song and stated that there was going to be a baptism. He called the little girl to be baptized to the front with him. She was a cute little girl, about ten years old, with blonde hair and blue eyes. Her smile was big and beautiful. Pastor Jim shared that baptism is a personal proclamation of faith in Christ, and he asked her if she understood that she was making a life decision that would change the course of her life.

She said excitedly, "Yes, sir, I do understand who He is."

"Do you believe that Jesus Christ is Lord of all?" he asked her.

"Yes, sir, I do."

"And why have you chosen to be baptized?"

"'Cause I want to promise myself to Him and know more about Him." Her sentence was like an arrow to my heart. Cupid's arrow.

"Okay, let's do this, then." Pastor Jim said as he led her to the baptismal room behind the glass.

I sat quietly in my seat, feeling as though He were holding my hand, walking me through my own beautiful memories, reminding me of who I was: a good girl who loved Jesus, not the filthy girl who left town covered in shame.

The splashing sound of the water brought me back to the present as the little girl was dunked under the water, making the cleansing complete.

The message was preached, and church ended. I ran into

another friend, Rachael, whom I recognized immediately because she had not changed one bit. We hugged and planned to do a lunch date that week. Being a little sidetracked, I knew I needed to find Mr. Cartway and ask him the question I'd been dying to ask him. Before I could finish the thought, I saw him by the door getting ready to leave.

Practically running up to him, I said, "Mr. Cartway, would you consider meeting with me? I would love more information on what happened oh so long ago. So much of my memory is gone, probably from blocking it all out, but I have questions. And, well, you are probably the only person I've been able to actually talk to that would be able to answer some of the questions I have had for all these years. I am not out to cause trouble; I just want some answers ..." I finished, unsure if I said it all the right way.

"Well, sure, just call my office in the morning and we'll get ya scheduled in," he said. I wasn't sure if it was reluctance or curiosity, but something made him hesitate and that made me nervous.

"Okay, great! I'll see you soon," I said, and walked out of the church.

*Did he really just agree to meet with me? Am I finally going to get some answers! What do I want to ask him? All I know is I'd better get in before he changes his mind. I don't think I can handle more letdowns and unanswered questions!*

Monday morning I wrestled with calling. As excited as I was at the prospect of having answers, I was also terrified at meeting the man who was responsible for getting my rapists off. He was the reason for the injustice. The wrestling match went on all day. Tuesday morning rolled around, and I still had not made the call. *What am I so afraid of?* Wednesday morning, as I drove to meet Rachael for lunch, I called and made the appointment for Thursday morning at ten.

I was in shock during the short drive over to Wendy's restaurant, where my friend and I were meeting for lunch. *They had scheduled the appointment, so it must really be happening! He didn't back out or tell the receptionist to relay to me that he couldn't meet with me. This is what I was expecting, a letdown. Was I finally going to get some answers to the age-old question of why?*

To be emotionally present with Rachael, I had to let it all go because I didn't want to miss the chance to reconnect with my long-lost friend. Of course, she asked me why I left so many years ago. When I told her, she cried and said she had no idea. I was beginning to believe that *they* really didn't know.

What was refreshing was that she opened up to me and shared her life with me. I loved that so much because it wasn't all about me! It was uplifting to be let into someone else's life story. We decided to meet at church together later on in the evening for Bible study.

After lunch, I figured I'd hit the library. It was the perfect place to begin writing this book ... and maybe smell a book or two! Smelling books is weird, I know. I can't help it, but it's something I've always done. I don't know how I learned it; I just know that a book's smell is comforting to me.

Taking a deep breath, I stood at the entrance with both doors held open, immediately feeling the surge of comfort. The place looked (and smelled) exactly the same. I had found my safe haven again, just like when I was a kid. Some days, as a kid, I'd go there just to sit and be alone, away from everyone else, and read. Mostly I loved just being there, surrounded by books. I didn't even have to read to enjoy the library. But always, without fail, I dreamed there. I dreamed of someday having my own book on the shelves.

As I walked through the small library, I wondered if my spot was still intact. Turning the corner from the adult fiction section and into the young adult fiction, there it was, my little cubby nook where I'd hung out with Nancy Drew, the Hardy Boys, Judy Blume, and V. C. Andrews. It had not even been slightly rearranged. It was as if they were all waiting for me to walk in, crouch down, and visit. So I did.

When the nostalgia wore off, I found a spot at a table, took out my laptop, and began typing. The words flew out of me. It was as if my story had been here, in this room of words, waiting for me to unleash it. All it took was my opening the door and walking in.

I wrote for a few hours, and every once in a while, I'd stop and pause to take in the moment of living my dream. Overwhelmed with accomplishment, I decided that I wanted to celebrate with ice cream. A peanut butter Blizzard from Dairy Queen sounded amazing.

Pulling into the Dairy Queen parking lot, I realized that this building used to be Burger Queen (Burger King's counterpart), and the memory instantly appeared without warning.

In 1981, while I was going through the three-month rape trial, my sister and I were at Burger Queen one day. We were sitting outside having a burger (a rare treat for us), and the police came up to us and interviewed us. It was completely inappropriate, and I remember being embarrassed and mortified. It's one of the memories I *didn't* block out. I felt as if everyone could hear them asking me about vaginas and penises and why I was where I was that night. It was wrong on so many levels.

The name of the business had changed from Burger Queen to Dairy Queen, so not by much, but it was the same building. There were still outside tables, probably the same ones. It all looked exactly how I remembered it. Feelings of anxiety started to arise within me. My heart started beating so fast that it hurt. My stomach was cramping, and I knew I had to gain control or else I'd be in a full-blown panic attack.

Something rose from deep within me.

*This is not going to own me again.*

Closing my eyes, I allowed the memory to come again and intentionally sat in the chair I thought I had sat in as a thirteen-year-old.

*I am going to eat my ice cream, and no one is going to get me this time!*

Again something rose from somewhere deep within, and I realized I had the power to change my memory. In counseling, I had learned of visual imagery as a way of battling anxiety. I started envisioning my sister and me there that day. I envisioned the cop coming up to us and interviewing us, just as it really happened. Then I envisioned my adult self approaching that cop and telling him that he was way out of line and that we didn't have to answer his questions. Then I took my sister by the hand and we left the table. I told the cop if he had a problem with me to take it up with his supervisor.

I was empowered, and the intensity of that old memory was instantly broken. As I sat in that chair eating my ice cream, I felt free. I had claimed victory over a horrible memory.

The ice cream was delicious as I marveled in my freedom. It was then that an older couple came up to me and asked if they could sit with me.

*Um, sure, there are only five other tables, but yeah, sit with me.*

"Sure, have a seat!" I heard myself say.

As the couple went to sit down, they introduced

themselves to me: Bill and Regina. My heart stopped. Anger and confusion engulfed me.

On the night of the rape, I was with four other girls and four boys. We had all been drinking, and the plan was for all of us girls to go stay the night at Monica Greyson's house. We went to her house at the end of the night, but for whatever reason, Monica's mother said I was not welcome in her home. She said that I was too drunk to stay there and for me to "get off her porch." I was afraid to go home and get into trouble, so I begged her to let me stay there, but she screamed at me to leave. I left her porch and started walking. The four boys picked me up, brought me to one of their grandma's vacant home, and took turns raping me all night long.

Her face has been embedded in my brain for all these years. Her name was Regina Greyson. *No frickin' way. This cannot be her ... I have to know.*

"Hi there, Regina and Bill. What's your last name?" I asked, hoping I sounded calm.

"Why, my name is Greyson, Regina Greyson."

Numbness so big engulfed me. Fear so profound encircled me. I was sitting next to one of the scariest and crassest people I had ever met. Never in my wildest dreams did I imagine that I'd be face-to-face with this woman. But here I was. And I was as scared as if I were thirteen all over again.

I turned from her and started praying quietly. My mind went crazy. I hoped my body could hold it together.

*What do I do with this, God? What do you want from me? Why did you put this woman in front of me? Why, oh why, and what do you want me to do here? Faith, not fear. Can I pull her toward me and scream in her face? Can I please just scream in her face? Pleassse ... Or pull her hair? Or do you want me to be nice? Why do you want me to be sitting here right now? Faith, not fear.*

*It's not working. Lord, help me.*

There wasn't a quick answer to this prayer, just silence.

We all sat there quietly. They didn't ask my name. They didn't talk to me, and I didn't talk to them. God apparently wasn't speaking either because I did *not* know what to do.

I decided just to wait. If they started asking who I was or where I was from or anything, I honestly did not know what I was going to say or do.

"Well, what's yourn' name?" Bill asked in his country kind of way.

"I'm Abigail." I was terrified to say my last name.

"Well, where ya from, girl? I aint' never seen ya around these parts," he stated.

"California." I think I was still eating my ice cream. I was trying to look normal but felt as if I had lost touch with reality.

Regina sat in her chair with her legs crossed, smoking her cigarette and looking off in the distance, ignoring my existence. She seemed cold and distant, but maybe that was just my perception of her.

Another older gentlemen walked up and started a conversation with me. I quickly caught on to the fact that this was their local hangout and this was probably their regular table. I was intruding on their space, not the other way around.

I had to turn around and away from Regina to talk with the newly arrived man, and he was a welcomed distraction as I wondered how to get out of this situation. I could have just gotten up and walked away. Maybe I stayed because I desperately wanted answers. Maybe it was a deeply rooted resentment toward myself that kept me sitting there acting like one of *them*. I really don't know how I sat in that chair for so long, though.

Finally, the second gentleman shifted into a different seat and I was forced to see her again. We sat there chatting it up about the weather, mowing country lawns, truck driving, and the economy. The shock was turning to anger, and boy, was it burning inside of me!

At one point, I actually did envision smacking the old lady across the face.

I sat there calm and silent, looking at her, daring her with my eyes to recognize me.

She started talking to the man she was with, still ignoring me. She talked about her children. These children of hers were the ones who cornered me in the school bathrooms during the trial and then chased me home. So much of my fear was directly connected to this family circle that she was referring to in her conversation.

Finally, Bill asked me, "So who are ya kin here in town?"

"My grandfather is Hank Deckert," I said, somehow managing not to let my voice sound as shaky as I felt on the inside.

Regina's mouth dropped, and she instantly touched my arm and squeezed it. She pulled me in close but didn't say a word. Not. One. Word. It was my nightmare all over again, that face so close to mine. I flinched but then looked her straight in the eyes.

I said, "I'm Abigail Blue, Hank's granddaughter. You know me, and I know you.

The look on her face said that she knew who I was. But like the good ole unspoken country way of doing things, she jumped back in her chair and just stared at me.

And I stared back.

She said, "Well, I know that ole' Hank Deckert. He is a stupid ole fool."

This time I grabbed her arm and pulled her close, saying, "The word 'stupid' and Hank Deckert do not go in the same sentence. He is the most honorable man I know."

And then I froze.

For whatever reason, I had nothing more in me. I don't know if the fear was overwhelming or if it was just one of those situations in life where shock takes over and you don't know what to do next, but I froze and didn't know what else to say. It was then that I knew to go.

As I walked away, I saw her pull Bill in close to her. He looked as if he was hearing something juicy, and I'm sure it was all kinds of gossip about me. He appeared to be engrossed in whatever she was saying, and I pulled away in my car and out of the parking lot.

Within minutes, I was on the side of the road, shaking and crying. Feelings of failure hit me hard. I had not stood up for myself. I had lost the words, my voice, again. I sat on the side of the road and sobbed. Once I could think straight again, I called a friend in California and had her talk me through the next few minutes. I was able to get grounded and drive again.

I just didn't know where to go. Church sounded good. I remembered that I was supposed to meet Rachael there for Bible study, so I drove there and waited for her. The few minutes in my car helped me pull it together, just in time for more intensity to rush over me. However, this time it was the good kind!

Ms. Margaret and I reconnected this night. She was easy to recognize. She still had the same black hair and big grin that welcomed anyone into any room. When I was a child, Ms. Margaret was my Brownie troop leader, my

Sunday school teacher, and she worked at the elementary school. She meant a lot to me as a child. I had never realized what an impact she had on my life until all these years later, at this moment, seeing her while I was in such a vulnerable state of mind. I had always looked up to her. Seeing her and reconnecting with her replaced the anxiety and stress with comfort and acceptance. She asked me what I'd been doing since being in town, and I told her I'd seen some friends and that today I went to the library and started writing a book. I told her about my library excursion and how fun it was to begin writing there. She knew how much I loved the library as a kid, so she got it. She was curious, though, and asked, "Where'd you go all those years ago, honey?"

As we stood outside the church, a stoic brick building that held so many good memories for me, I shared my story with her.

She cried and said she couldn't believe it. I told her I was meeting with the defense lawyer from the case and would be writing about my experience.

She replied with, "What kind of lawyer would get any boy off after doing *that* to you?" I couldn't tell her it was the deacon at her church and that I was meeting him the next morning.

The morning couldn't come fast enough. I tossed and turned most of the night. I was anxious and curious to see what was going to happen at the appointment with Mr. Cartway. My intention was to make a list of questions, but I couldn't even manage to do that. I was dumbfounded by the idea of being face-to-face with this man and actually talking about the rape—the subject that had been pushed aside and swept under a rug for so many years. It was surreal to me to imagine getting it out in the open. A big part of me wanted to put on my running shoes and run clear back to California.

My mind was blank. I didn't know what to ask and I was terrified.

Setting my fear aside, I decided to focus on how ecstatic I was to talk someone who knew *something* and could acknowledge the reality of what really happened and why it ended the way it did.

Turning from the country road and onto Main Street, only blocks from my destination, my cell rang with a Kentucky area code and all my hope flew out the window. There would be no answers from Mr. Cartway. I knew before I even answered the call.

"Hello?" I said, with only a tiny glimmer of hope remaining. I hoped I was wrong and that it was someone else, anyone else but him.

"Hello, Abigail. This is Calvin Cartway. Listen, I hate to do this to you so last minute, but I cannot meet with you."

*I knew it.*

He continued. I listened. Hope definitely deflated.

"Listen, it's not ethical for me to meet with you, and I'm really sorry. And besides, I can't recollect anything about this particular case. Also, I have to consider that this family still lives in town. You seem like a nice girl, and I will pray for your closure in this area."

Maybe I thought that by meeting me, he would move from the *they* team to *my* team! His cancelling this meeting cemented himself as a *they*!

"Okay, Mr. Cartway, I completely respect your professionalism and thank you for calling me before I arrived there at your office. I was not meeting you for closure. I am whole," I lied. (Or did I? I wasn't too sure.) "What I wanted from our meeting was the simple facts about the case because I don't have any memory of the court case. I've tried to get the court transcript, but to no avail. If you have any other suggestions as to where I can get information, please tell me."

"I don't know what to tell you, but have a nice day and God bless ya," he said.

And as I slammed the flip phone shut, a door slammed shut as well, in my face, never to be opened again.

Instead of self-pity, something else rose up. All of a sudden, all the questions that I couldn't come up with were replaced with answers from deep within myself. *I know who is my judge. I know who my identity maker is. And it certainly isn't Calvin Cartway. Or anyone else for that matter.*

*The answers were within me.*

*Somewhere.*

Falling back to everything I had been reading in my Bible study, the belief arose. *I am who God says I am. Period.*

*Then why do they matter so much to me?*

This inner battle had been raging on and on. The information I had been reading in the Bible wasn't really sinking in if I was still walking around needing the approval of others, *was it?*

Confused, I kept driving, just as I always had, because after all, I was a born runner. I was just so tired.

Because Uncle Hank was going to go with me to see Mr. Cartway, I had to let him know we didn't need to meet. We decided to go have breakfast and hang out at Pop's afterward. Uncle Hank suggested we didn't talk about the lawyer because it would upset Pop and Granny Nil. "It's all so upsetting to Daddy, you know. Your mother never even told him about it. He found out by reading it in the local newspaper."

*What! Pop had found out about the rape in the local newspaper? My mother never told him?*

The compulsion attached to the questions put me in a

bad mood. I wanted to be done with this whole situation already, but a new battle ensued. *Why couldn't I let it all go?* was matched with *Why didn't my mother tell my grandparents?* They were practically my guardians back then. Maybe she was just ashamed of me and that is why it was kept so quiet. I really didn't know. I just knew it really pissed me off. And then the humdinger of all questions: *What* was *in the local newspaper back then?*

It didn't take long to find the answer.

With the library right around the corner, I walked over to see if I could find old newspaper information. Within an hour, I had pulled up the microfiche for the newspaper for January 1981. And there it was.

It was a small article that said that a nineteen-year-old male brought a thirteen-year-old female across the state line, purchased beer, and brought her back into Kentucky, along with two females and three other males. Later the thirteen-year-old went back with the three boys and was supposedly raped. The other two boys said that Broderick and the thirteen-year-old went into the other room to "sit" for ten minutes; and when Broderick found out the thirteen-year-old filed rape charges the next day, he turned himself in. The other two girls said that the thirteen-year-old had said she didn't know who she had sex with and that she wanted to drop charges, but her mother wouldn't let her. Graham Broderick's attorney, Calvin Cartway, said, "I think the jury followed the evidence and the law presented in the case. All of the witnesses, including the medical testimony, supported the position taken by the defendant from the filing of these charges through the end of the case. Calvin Cartway added, "I was pleased with the results, and I'm sure Graham Broderick and his family are also gratified with the jury's verdict of acquittal."

Unbelief made me reread it several times, followed by

the same reaction each time: shock. There were so many misstatements in this article.

I didn't have *much* memory of that night, but I had enough memory to know that what they did to me lasted the whole night, not ten minutes! It was dark when it started. I know that for certain Graham was the last one to violate me. I was 100 percent coherent and alert when it was his turn. The other two were like foggy dreams. Thank God I didn't feel it as much, for those other two violated me in ways that would make a lot of women cringe.

I could understand how the defendants would claim their lies to be truth. What truly upset me about the article was that it said the medical testimony supported the defendant.

"All of the witnesses, including the medical testimony, supported the position taken by the defendant from the filing of these charge through the end of the case," was what the article had read.

How was that possible? I remembered that medical exam! I remembered what the doctor had said.

Sitting there in the chair at the microfiche machine with closed eyes, I was instantly the traumatized teen and in the emergency room having my first gynecological exam the morning after the rape. Mom had come home from work and had found me in my bedroom. She found out what happened and rushed me to the hospital, where she stood next to me, holding my hand as I lay on the exam table with my legs in stirrups. Opened up and on display once again. I felt gross as I was poked and prodded.

"You were a virgin, correct?" the doctor had asked me, breaking through the blackness of closed eyes and horrific shame, making me answer her.

"Yes," I said, willing my eyes to stay shut.

"Does this hurt?" she asked as she poked my insides.

"No." Even though everything did. Every place she touched hurt. Every. Fiber. Of. My. Being. Hurt.

"I don't see how. It looks very painful" I remember her saying.

I bit my lip, and the tears stayed at bay. The idea of the dam breaking loose terrified me. I was so confused. So scared. So embarrassed. I kept my eyes closed as she finished her exam.

A few minutes later, she said, "Okay, I'm done with my exam." And she gently pushed my knees back together.

The doctor looked at my mom and said, "She has several abrasions and bruises inside, but I don't see anything that would be permanent damage. We took some samples for the lab, but since she had a long bath, I'm sure there isn't much there. She has obviously had rough sex and is no longer a virgin. And of course there is the possibility of sexual disease and maybe even pregnancy."

My heart felt as though it had stopped beating, and I held my breath. Her words suffocated me. I couldn't hear anymore. I closed my eyes and my ears because it was safer in the dark.

Opening my eyes, the library came into focus, as did the article still on the screen. The initial shock wore off, and I knew I couldn't look at it anymore. Looking at it only angered me more. I was able to take the microfiche out of the machine and return it to the librarian, after which I hightailed it out of there.

I was done.

I couldn't wait to fly out the next day.

It was time to be done with all this. *There are no answers here, just more questions. I'm tired of this, and I'm just ... well ... done. I want to go home to my husband. Please, God, let me have a husband whose arms I can fall into when I get there.*

# Chapter 10

# *The Injustice of it All*

Returning home, anger consumed me as I slipped into the abyss of depression resulting from yet another relapse by Matt while I was away from him. Into the inpatient rehab he went, and I kept our business going by hiring a new technician. I did my best to answer the phones; however, customer service had become a challenge.

My nerves were shot, and it was hard to talk to anyone, much less customers, without my voice sounding shaky and insecure.

*How do I do this?*

The injustice from my past was beginning to pale in comparison to the injustice currently going on in my life. All strength was gone, and defeat had set in. Not only were there no answers—just crazy dead-end loopholes, keeping my story from getting written—but I also felt abandoned by my husband and was beginning to feel distanced by my God.

Coping looked like overworking, overeating, and under exercising. Exhaustion was my constant companion. And it only got worse as I sat on my couch and watched TV, which is where, once again, God met me right where I was.

One day, immersed in depression and self-pity, I watched a program about a man who was on trial for sexual assault. He was facing several counts of rape from various women. He wasn't physically violent. He was manipulative, and he drugged them. He raped them in their unconscious state. He was acquitted on all counts. The women were smeared with character assaults, and they questioned their own choices. Some battled with the thoughts of "Is it rape?" "I wasn't killed." "I wasn't even physically hurt." Ultimately, they were powerless to the man who drugged them and powerless to the system. The powerlessness and self-doubt were also constant companions for me now.

The Lord told me a long time ago to talk, to testify again. Not in a court of law, but to others. To others who struggle with the injustice of having been raped and not acknowledged in a court of law—to testify to the ones who were not believed.

The Lord told me to write a book about it. I told Him I couldn't do that. I told Him I didn't know what to say and that I don't know how to write something that *big*. He told me to talk of the freedom one can only receive through Him. He told me to talk about how He doesn't make any "junk" and that our true identity is in Him. It does not come from what others believe about us. He told me that not everyone gets justice in this world. And that injustice does *not have to take away our freedom or our identity.* I am who *HE* says I am. He says He believes in me. He has shown me all these things, and I want to truly believe and walk in these truths.

I suppose that I'm afraid *I* won't be believed again. It's a very strong and real fear, one that has kept me from moving forward in this area. The fear of not being believed keeps me from believing that I can do this! That is so ironic.

Sometimes my unbelief paralyzes me.

Well, after I watched this man acquitted on TV, I realized I needed to tell my story before it was too late. Women are out there living with injustice, walking around in defeat, believing they are the condemned. I didn't want to die failing in this job that God had given me to do by not doing it! At least if I tried, I couldn't completely fail.

Anger rose up from within. "Let's get serious about this!" I said aloud to myself.

I stood up and looked in the big mirror that hung above the couch. "Where are you?" I asked the reflection, talking to the author in me that Laura, the court attendant, had identified. "Why do you keep quitting?"

I remembered the little boy who sang that day in the courthouse. I began singing the words to the song that quieted my beating heart that day.

*Yes, Jesus loves me ... Yes, Jesus loves meeee ...*

My heartbeat starting calming down.

*Yes. Jesus. Loves. Me.*

Continuing the conversation with myself, I said, "Let's do this. I cannot live another day trapped in this silence." But two hours later, I still couldn't find the paperwork. It had been safely tucked away in my laptop case for three years. I would get it out occasionally and look at it, wondering what to do with it. I had seen it every time I went to use my laptop. I'd always known exactly where it was. But, now, I needed it and it wasn't there. I searched every place I could think of. I searched all the places it shouldn't have been. I simply couldn't find it.

Dropping to my knees in my closet, faced with the ultimate loss for words, actual words this time, I hit a wall of sorts and questioned the purpose of it all.

*How could I tell the story without the jury list?* But then it occurred to me: *What did I need it for, anyway?*

The list had its purpose. It led me on a journey that I otherwise would not have walked down. It had guided me. Maybe it served its purpose and was just holding me back, somehow keeping me from writing!

*Maybe I need to stop expecting God to give me every single word.*

*Maybe I needed to let go … Maybe I needed …*

The sound of the ringing phone interrupted my thoughts; it was Anne's number on the screen.

"Hey, what's up?" I knew she had to hear the irritation in my voice.

"Well, I just thought I would let you know that Judge Lovell died last night," she said matter-of-factly.

I didn't know what to say. I didn't want to believe her words. Within seconds, I knew the impact of this for me. It was selfish to think of myself as I heard of someone else's death. But that is exactly what I did. I thought about the last time I was there and drove right past his office. I thought about how I knew I should have gone in and interviewed him. He could have had all the answers that I wanted. He could have known why the jury didn't believe me.

And now he was gone. I felt a sort of death wash over me, along with the returning desperation and despair.

"Oh, okay," I mustered. "I can't talk, Anne. I'll call you later." And I hung up on my sister.

She knew that I had to be devastated, but she could have no idea that I was literally in a battle over it right before she called. The letting go forgotten, I clung to the desperation of gaining control over it … something … anything.

Frantically, I searched for the court paperwork again, to no avail. But wait! I remembered that Leroy had copies. Panic set in, and I quickly logged onto Facebook to see if Leroy was online. He was!

"Hey, Leroy," I typed.

"Hey, girl, what's up?" he typed back.

"I'd like to get the copies you have of that court paperwork." I couldn't type the words fast enough. I was frantic.

"Well, that's going to be a problem, as they were accidentally shredded ... I am so sorry."

Hope faded. The judge had died, the paperwork was missing, and I felt as if I'd blown it and that I'd never have the answers. I'd never have the words.

Despair settled in even deeper.

*What held me back from talking to Judge Lovell while I was there? How did I lose such important paperwork?*

Procrastination slapped me in the face, weighty and painful. And I knew that it was all my doing. I shouldn't have waited. I shouldn't have been so lackadaisical.

Needing to clear my mind, I hopped in my car and headed to the beach. I wanted to scream in anger. Instead, I walked silently along the beach. The ebb and flow of the ocean mellowed my mind somewhat. I was able to begin to calm down and pray. I think it was praying. I mean, I was talking with God, hoping He was there listening.

It's rare I can bring my anger to Him, but I did that day. I was pissed off and confused, and I articulated it to Him without any fear of being struck down.

*Why did you bring me this far, God? I have not received any justice. I have messed up and lost it all. The paperwork is gone, the person with answers is now dead, and I'm left with no justice. Why did you make me go back there? For what? I don't know how to write this story, especially with this ending!*

"Your justice is my joy within you." It was instantly etched upon me like a tattoo.

I didn't fully understand it, yet intuitively I knew that it was *the* answer I needed. Somehow I knew I had been given a key to my healing. The confusion lifted a tiny bit. Just knowing that God spoke to me was huge, but not having a clue what it meant started me asking even more questions.

*How come I don't feel this joy you say is in me, and how on earth is that justice?*

Later that week, the impact of God's voice was quieted by my uncle's voice on the phone as he told me that Pop had broken his pelvic bone and he was now in the nursing home, where he would more than likely be the rest of his life.

I immediately got on the phone with the nursing home and insisted on talking with my grandfather.

"I can't … stay here. I need … to go home. They don't feed me here," Pop said. The crackle in his voice reminded me of the unfamiliar tears I saw in him at his birthday celebration a few years earlier. This time there was no question that there were tears. Pop sounded more like a child than a man, powerless to the decisions others were making for him. His devastation was apparent, and I desperately wanted to help him. I *needed* to help him.

Hoping my desperation wasn't in my tone, I replied to him. "Pop, I know this is hard. I know you want to be home. I'm sorry that you are in so much pain. You are going to be okay." *How must it feel to know you are dying in a short amount of time?*

"I don't want to be here. I just want to go home," he said softly.

He didn't deserve to die like this. Why couldn't he be home? I made a mental note to ask my uncle or talk to the nurses to find out what, if anything, could be done to let him go home. If this truly was the end of his life, he deserved to be home, and if I could do anything to make that happen, how great would that be?

Again I reassured him. "Pop, I know you don't want to be there, and I'm so sorry."

"Can you come take me home, Abigail?" He spoke so softly that I could barely hear him.

This man had never asked a thing from me, or probably from anyone else, for that matter. His request had weight. "I don't know, Pop, but let me see what I can do."

"Please. I'm begging." And he hung up.

My whole body felt heavy, really heavy. He and I were on such similar journeys; we both were desperate to be home.

*Was there really anything I could do to help my beloved grandfather?*

I decided to call and check with the nurse to see if he was eating okay. I could start there. Maybe I could arrange for Anne to go visit him and bring him whatever he wanted to eat. That would be a start. Once I got the nurse on the phone, I quickly found out that there was an option. The nurse said that he could in fact go home if he got himself from the bed to his chair on his own. If he could master that, then they would release him to his own home, with home health care!

"Oh, this is so encouraging!" I exclaimed to the nurse. "Do you think it's a reasonable goal? I mean, do you think he can gain that kind of strength after such a traumatic injury at his age?" I asked her.

"Well, that will depend on him, of course. He would have to be persistent and he'd have to work awfully hard at it. But I think it is possible if he does everything we tell him to do."

"Will you transfer me over to him, please?" I couldn't wait to share the news with him.

"Sure thang ... Hang on ..."

After a few moments of silence, Pop was back on

the phone. "Yeees?" He sounded distant on the phone. I wondered if maybe he had the phone upside down or something. He sounded as though he were in a tunnel.

"Pop! It's me, Abigail, again. I have great news for you! Can you hear me?" I hoped my excitement would be catchy.

"I'm ... here."

"Pop, the nurse just told me that if you could do some things that they want you to do, that you can go home!" As I said the words, I realized that there could be a possibility of this bringing him further down if he failed at meeting their goal. I had to take the chance, though. He could at least try.

"Do what?" His voice became clearer.

"There's a chance you can go home, Pop! They want you to be able to work at getting stronger. If you can work with the physical therapist there, and you can get strong enough to get from your bed to your chair, then they will help you go home." I held my breath, waiting for his response.

"Do what? Get in my chair? I can't do that," he said flatly.

"Okay, I know you can't now, and it's okay if you can't at all. I just wanted to let you ..."

"But you are saying if I get strong enough to do that, then I can go home?" His voice was gaining some strength.

"Yes! That's exactly what I'm sayi—"

He interrupted. "I can do it. I will do anything to be home."

"I get it, Pop! And I will do anything to get you there."

He needed encouragement, and I wanted to be with him. I wanted to personally get him home. It would take several weeks to make this happen, but I was determined to help him.

My life was in total chaos (and powerlessness) because

of Matt's maddening addiction, but I could do *this*. I wanted to do this for my Pop!

Uncle Hank, Pop's legal guardian and next of kin, gave the go-ahead, and off to Kentucky I went.

Feelings of ultimate helplessness are evoked when I enter a nursing home. The hallways smell of despair. That odor has accompanied every nursing home I have ever stepped into, and I'd been in a few in my lifetime.

As a small kid, maybe seven or eight years old, I'd go to the nursing home where my mother worked as a nurse and I'd hold my nose. "Ewwwww. It smells like poop or something in here!" I said the first time I'd smelled it.

"Abigail, get your hand off your nose and don't say those things. The people here are sick, and their families can no longer care for them. Consider that they smell it too and that they don't like it either." my mother said, and a compassion for the elderly was birthed deep within me.

My heart had changed, but the smell had not. There was always an underlying stinkiness, despite the disinfectant.

The hallway was long, and the floor was squeaky clean. Each step made my presence known, although I didn't seem to be alerting anyone. The walls were lined with patients in wheelchairs, many permanently hunched over, with their eyes only looking at their laps. Most of the eyes that did look up were vacant; only a few were inquisitive.

One man in particular caught my attention. He was extremely old and sat tall in his wheelchair, but his face was expressionless. He wore overalls and a flannel shirt. His baseball cap was as worn and weathered as he looked. He took his hat off and looked at it with curiosity. Maybe he couldn't read; I wasn't sure. Then he chuckled and returned his hat to his head. As I walked by him, I saw that it read World's Greatest Dad.

Across from him was a woman not much older than I; she appeared to have Down syndrome. When she noticed me, she almost lunged out of her chair as she reached for me, startling me. It scared me at first, and I jumped, but then she immediately settled back in and starting singing "Amazing Grace."

The remainder of the patients didn't move as I squeaked past them, looking for room A47.

As I stepped inside the dark hospital room, I saw a shadowy figure in a wheelchair by the window, hunched over. *Is that Pop, sleeping?* He looked so small. It couldn't be him, but this was his private room.

"Pop?" I said quietly.

His head popped up, and he looked back to see who was approaching him.

"It's me, Abigail," I whispered, not wanting to startle him.

"Do what?" he asked. *Yep, that's Pop.* He would say that when he didn't understand something.

Gently touching his shoulder, not sure if he comprehended that is was me yet, I said, "Hi, it's Abigail, Pop. I'm here."

His shoulders began shaking, and for a brief moment, I thought he might be having a seizure or something, and then I realized he was weeping.

There was no mistaking his emotion this time. I wasn't standing across a room wondering. I was right there with him. I held him while he cried.

Eventually, he calmed down and pushed me back a little bit so he could clearly see me. "Thank you," he whispered as he reached for my hand. "I know you are here to help me get back home. I've been anxiously waiting for you, and I can't thank you enough for sacrificing your own time and doing this. It means everything to me, and I love you, my precious granddaughter."

Letting go of his hand and embracing him in a tight hug, I couldn't hold my tears back for another moment. "I love you too, Pop," I said as I clung to him for dear life.

We sat together for a little while, and then he told me to "go on my way" so he could get to bed. He had work to do starting the next day. As I walked out of the room and back down the hallway, I knew without any doubt that I was supposed to be here.

Beginning the next day and over the next month, he did the hard work and got himself strong enough to get from his bed to his chair on his own. And that meant he got to go home.

During that time, I spent most of my time at the nursing home with him, and I got to know some of the other patients there. I learned that Bill, the "World's Greatest Dad," was an Alzheimer's patient who knew nothing at all, except that he was a great daddy to his kids. Somehow you can tell by looking in his eyes that the title was well earned. I learned that Patty, the amazing and graceful singer, was reaching out so she could kiss my hand every time she saw me—she just wanted someone to sit next to her and listen to her song.

Another patient, Carrie, walked the hallway each day, always in a big hurry. Occasionally she would come into Pop's room, stop at his bedside, and stare at him as if trying to remember him. The nurses told me Pop looked like her husband, who had been there every day for her until recently, when he passed away.

Pop ended up getting a roommate, Marlan. He was blind and paralyzed from the neck down, and still he managed to smile every time I entered the room. He loved Elvis and really knew his music. He loved to talk to whomever gave him the time to do so.

There were others that I didn't get to know, but I was no longer afraid. Getting Pop home had turned into a priceless adventure for both of us.

# Chapter 11

# *Allured*

Little Mountain, October 2013

*Left or right?*

As I sat at the stop sign, I realized once again that I did not know which way to turn. Here I was again, *lost*. The accomplishment of knowing that Pop was home was satisfying. He had persevered, and he fought hard to get home! I had done exactly what I had set out to do: get him home.

He showed up to physical therapy three times a day, and he got stronger. Along with my other family members, I encouraged him and cheered him on. We made sure his spirits were strong, and we gave back to him everything he had ever given to us: encouragement and a strong sense of empowerment.

And now, just a week into his being home, I couldn't for the life of me understand why I was *really* here.

Being gone from Matt and our life in San Diego for two months was choosing to let the chips fall where they may with him. I was too exhausted to try to hold our life together on my own anymore. I thought that by coming and helping Pop, well, I could at least have purpose. It all felt so off at that moment.

Now that he was settled, safe, and sound at home, the last thing I expected was to be rejected by them. I knew there would be resistance. It was unrealistic to believe that one could be enduring such hardship and loss of physical ability without experiencing a good amount of anger. I knew from prior experience with the elderly that there was potential for the anger to be directed at me, but I wasn't prepared for the verbal confrontation that went down with Nilda.

She told me I was bossy and controlling. I told her she was mean, and then they *both* wanted me to leave. Honestly, I don't think she ever really wanted me there to begin with.

I should have been home in California, trying to cope with being an empty nester with kids going off to college. Instead, I sat at the stop sign in Little Mountain, *lost*. My only two choices were to go left or to go right. A left turn would take me to Mom and Anne's town of Alba. (They had the stomach flu, so that was not an option for me.) A right turn would get me to the highway leading out of Little Mountain and into the next town, Cumberland. If I simply went straight, I'd end up in some poor soul's driveway.

I decided to turn right and get to the highway. There were some beautiful cornfields along the way, and I'd always wanted to photograph them. Maybe losing myself behind my camera would help. I could at least rest my brain cells from thinking about all the problems for a while.

Driving along Highway 29, I managed to capture a handful of images with my camera before I realized that I really needed just to *be*. I needed to sleep in a bed, not on a couch; I was so tired of being away from the comforts of my own home. Even before getting here several weeks ago, I'd been living out of my trunk and on someone's couch for about two weeks, and it all just weighed down on me in that moment …

What I really needed was to cry it out. I needed privacy and a place to surrender the tears.

I drove toward the neighboring town of Cumberland, where there were more possibilities for finding a reasonably priced and clean motel. The thirty-minute drive was exhausting, and the uncertainty of destination was despairing. I kept asking myself, *Where do I belong?*

As I exited the highway and came upon the town of Cumberland, I saw a sign that read The Lost Lodge. My heart knew I needed to check that out; however, I kept driving because I assumed it had to be more expensive than the "leave the light on" motels I'd become accustomed to.

I kept driving down the long stretch of road, both sides marked with store after store. *Finally, some civilization!* When you go from Big City, California, to Extremely Small Town, Kentucky, it's a culture shock. *Maybe I can even find a good cup of hot tea here.* (Starbucks doesn't exist there, and this had been a long visit!) The only place in Little Mountain that afforded me a hot cup of tea was McDonald's, and they had run out as of yesterday morning. As coffee is to most people, my tea, English breakfast style, is my morning necessity!

I drove all the way down Highway 29 to the end of Cumberland. From my cell phone, I called every motel that I drove past; the prices shocked me. They were more expensive than the ones in California! I decided to drive over to The Lost Lodge. *Why not? They might be the same price. Who knows?*

I pulled into the office area of the lodge, and I wasn't sure how I felt about it. The office was tucked away in the trees, and all I saw were cabins lined up and snuggled into the immense forest behind it. I didn't see any motel rooms, just cabins.

A woman approached me. "How may I help ya?" She seemed surprised to have a customer. I decided to act coy and feel out the situation before making it obvious that I was alone in search of a room. I felt too vulnerable.

I said, "We're considering a family reunion here, and I'd like to check out the place and get pricing."

"No problem, hon. When are ya thinkin'?"

"The end of November," I lied.

She gave me the weekly pricing, and I thanked her. As I walked away, figuring it out in my head, I realized that it was rather affordable, more affordable than the Super 8 down the road. *Hmm, I wonder if I could stay here for the week.*

"Go on and drive around and check out the place. You'll love it," she said with a cheerful smile.

I started down the gravel road and drove farther onto the property. There were about twenty cabins and a few bigger houses, all forming a circle. The sound of my tires on the gravel road somehow made me smile. It reminded me of a recent summer memory of Matt and me leaving the county fair. We had had such a great day together, and I remember leaving the fair so connected and in love with my husband. Even though I was currently terribly sad over our separation, feelings of contentment overwhelmed me. *It's the small things in life, I guess.*

When I came out of my county fair memory, I realized I was smack dab in the middle of a forest, a wilderness. I had driven halfway through the lodge property and I was at the bottom of the hill, about to go back up the other side. I was struck by the majesty and awe surrounding me.

Stopping my car, I sat in the driver's seat and stared up at the trees, so tall and stout, all around me. Shrubs of various plants full with rich greenery surrounded me. I took in the smell of the rich soil and composting leaves. The sound of the crackling branches was crisp as the wind whistled through my car. The light filtering through the tops of the trees enthralled me.

Suddenly, I remembered a Scripture (Hosea 2:14) that I had read recently: "Therefore I am now going to allure her; I will lead her into the wilderness and speak tenderly to her." This Scripture had been underlined, circled, and highlighted in my Bible time after time, always during one of my husband's gnarly relapses. But never had it had so much significance as right now in this moment. Never had I felt so cradled and tenderly spoken to. Peace overwhelmed me, and I no longer felt lost.

God, my Abba, was speaking to me through the forest, the Kentucky wilderness that He had led me to.

The trees seemed to be saying to me, "I stand tall and mighty, protecting you from the heat." The deep and rich greenery seemed to speak a sort of purity into my being. The aroma of the dark soil told my soul that my foundation was solid. The branches sang into me a sense of hidden wonders yet to be found. And finally the filtering light tenderly whispered into my vulnerable, hurting heart, "I am."

I was afraid to move. I didn't want the moment to end. But I knew I had to go check in and get settled. I had a place to "be" … a place to rest.

I circled back to the office and told the woman that I'd like to stay the next week and asked if she could accommodate me. She said, "I'd be happy to, hon."

Nestled between the trees, my cabin had a rustic look to it. The green aluminum roof sort of matched the green moss all around the trees leading up to the sides of the cabin. The rocking chair on the front porch was waiting patiently for me, and the front light was on, as if to welcome me home.

The inside of the cabin was just as welcoming as the outside, with knotty pine walls and low ceilings. The living room was simple and furnished with only a couch, a chair, and a small coffee table. There was a table in the kitchen beside the stovetop and microwave for cooking, along with a full-size refrigerator. I breathed a sigh of relief as I noticed tea bags in a jar on the table. The bedroom had a private door and a beautiful view into the wilderness that I had so quickly fallen in love with.

Lying down on the bed and staring out the window and into the trees, tears welled up and I thought about stopping them. I was good at stopping the tears. I thought about getting up and making a cup of tea. I considered going for a walk or trying to read a book—anything but sit in the stillness.

They started slowly at first, with one tear trickling down my cheek, then another … and then another. I thought about unpacking. I felt another tear trickle down my cheek. I thought about Matt and what he was probably doing at that moment. The image in my head was too much to bear. Drugs always involved things a husband had no business doing. It was then that the tears were released. I fell on my face and sobbed uncontrollably for thirty minutes.

As my chest heaved in and out and I felt the gut-wrenching pain of abandonment, I emptied the tears onto the bed's comforter, and with each convulsing sob, I remembered.

I remembered every hurtful word and devastating act brought on by addiction. Every other sob would bring a beautiful picture of my husband's face when drugs didn't overtake him and he loved me with all his heart. I remembered our last weekend together and just how grateful we both were to be able to love so deeply. *How does this happen when things are so good?*

Finally, I was able to gather myself together and sit up. I looked out the window and noticed that the sky had also opened up and it had rained.

Perhaps God had cried with me.

It had not rained very much, just enough to bring the aroma of refreshment. Breathing in, I ingested the renewal. It was as if I could smell every wet leaf. I could even smell the droplets of rain resting on the mossy ground. I could smell the newness that comes for those few brief moments when the dirt is all washed away.

The trees were brighter and greener than just a half hour ago. The sounds were louder, clearer, as if the birds were chirping and the bugs were singing, taking on each others' language. Everything was crisp, clear, and made sense to me—everything except my heart—but to have any peace, I couldn't think. I simply had to just focus on the trees.

I'm no poet but something was being written as I allowed everything else to fall out of focus.

### An Orchestra of Trees

*Allured into the wilderness*
*Longing for a song*
*A tender promise I await*
*I am patient to belong.*

*Amongst the towering trees and fog*
*The thickening begins to clear*
*And the curtain rises*
*Taking with it, fear.*

*Directed by the wind*
*Is a symphony from above*
*Long Harmonic tones saying,*
*"Upright and true--I am rooted in love."*

*"In jubulance and joy, the birds sing of my unity*
*The leaves a festival of my grace dancing to the ground"*
*Twirling, spinning, landing...*
*The wind, a gentle trumpet's sound.*

*I'm the audience to His heartbeat*
*He whispers like the willow ...*
*"You have my joy within you*
*come, be still and know."*

The gentle wind lulled me to back sleep, and when I woke up the next morning, the window was still open. With my bed right up against the window, I adjusted my pillow to lean on the window sill.

Staring outside, the scene was just as enthralling as it was the evening before—except this morning brought a new gift: deer. They were standing in the middle of the forest, about one hundred feet from my cabin, and were completely unaware of my existence. I gasped as a fawn looked up and right into my eyes, letting me know *she* was aware of my presence. She continued to eat with no fear of me. The noise from another cabin close by startled the deer, and they all ran off. I lay there just looking off into the bushes they had run into. *Where did they go?*

Fighting the automatic reaction to jump up and go do *something*, I forced myself to lie on the bed and do *nothing*. Of course, tears found their way through the nothingness and I let them flow again.

All week I did that same thing. I cried while doing a lot of nothing. I didn't read, I didn't write, I didn't even talk to anyone. I kept occupied with the beauty on the property at The Lost Lodge. There was a swing in the middle of the property and a dock on the lake, so I spent my "not crying" time swinging and sitting on the dock, watching the birds.

By the end of the week, I had found another part of me. What I found was broken, but I also knew it was going to be okay.

With this assurance, I felt stronger and knew it was time to leave The Lost Lodge and go check on Pop and Nilda. I needed to make things right. I needed to get into their good graces and take care of them. They needed me, and I needed them.

And just like every other time I'd entered my grandfather's home, I was welcomed with opened arms. Nilda appreciated my apology for yelling back at her. I acknowledged that there was no excuse for my anger to be directed toward them. She acknowledged that she shouldn't have yelled at me either. "It's my fear talkin'," she admitted. "I'm not used to being taken care of."

Pop sat in his chair as Nilda and I cried and hugged each other tightly. We had an understanding in that moment; we understood and respected the beauty that was underneath the armor we both wore.

Much like Pop, who was doing well and settled in, I had to fight my way back home too —with or without my husband — I was ready and determined to be home. Matt had recently called to let me know he had finished his sixty-day program, and I agreed to try the marriage once again. I knew I would need to be in warrior mode. With determination, I knew I would need that same perseverance and grit that it took for Pop to make it.

It was there, at home with my husband, that I got the news that changed me forever.

From my journal

November 2013

*Last night I got a call that Pop had a heart attack*
*and was rushed to the hospital. The doctor said*
*he wasn't going to make it through this one.*
*I fell asleep in a sweet sadness that I wouldn't be*
*with him at the finish line. I fell asleep grateful that*
*I got to be a part of his journey here on earth.*
*I looked at the clock; it was 2:08 a.m. I'd awakened from*
*an intense dream about falling from an airplane and*
*landing at a waiting dock. I was wide-awake and had*
*the impression to pray for Pop. I prayed that he would not*
*suffer and asked the Lord to bring him escorts. I prayed for*
*peace and comfort ... however much Pop needed, to please*
*provide it. I asked Him to allow someone familiar, hopefully*
*my sister, to be with Pop when he took his last breath. I*
*asked Him to surround him with His angels. I prayed that*
*the Lord's angels would escort Pop during his exit from*
*this world, through whatever journey we experience in*
*between this earthly life and his entrance to be with God.*
*Please just not alone, Lord.*
*I prayed hard. I prayed long. I prayed*
*till I didn't have words left.*
*Then I prayed in the spirit.*
*I was praying in a rhythm that was redundant and had a*
*familiar structure, but now I don't remember the actual sound*
*of it. I remember being completely absorbed and lost in the*
*rhythm of the song my spirit was singing to God. With eyes*

*closed, I saw what looked like white silk material being blown by the wind, but so much more beautiful than silk. I was immersed in the softness. I felt light and lifted up and deep and warm within some sort of cocoon ... I actually wondered if I was dying. It was startling and beautiful. I remember thinking,*
Am I the one dying?

*I was lost in the experience, and then all of a sudden I wasn't lost in it anymore. It was done. I reached over and felt Matt's arm, reconnecting to reality. I was fully awake and didn't know what to do. What had just happened? I tried to go back to sleep. I was tossing and turning when the phone rang and my sister told me that she had just made it to the hospital five minutes before Pop passed away peacefully in his sleep, with her and Nilda by his side.*

*All I know right now is that my Abba Papa allowed me to journey beside my grandfather.*

# Chapter 12

# *Sticks and Stones, Lovey*

Little Mountain, Kentucky, April 2015

For a while now, I've been searching.

I've searched for the little girl I left lying at the rape scene, the mother who stayed in town, the grandparents' adoration that I so desperately missed, the friends who were waiting for me all these years—and so many other lost things.

I've searched and longed for all that I had lost along the way.

The search has been ongoing for someone or something to answer not just the *why* but the *who*.

*Who am I?*

This thing that happened to me defined every role I've ever played in life. It scarred the wife and mother in me. It stole the innocence that I had so desperately searched for, hoping to find the answers that would fill me back up, make me whole again. Actually, not *again*—but for the first time. I don't think I was whole to begin with.

I've searched for all these things because I've desperately wanted to heal.

Words are a part of that search. I think it's why I write. Finding the lost words is my goal. I've been searching for them for years, trying to find the ones that will heal. Trying to find the ones I need to say and the words that I quite possibly need to hear. I try to find the words to write, the ones that propel me full circle. Through my Gilgals.

The most recent words that I searched for were handwritten words that I began seeing in my mind about a month prior. I don't know where I was or what I was doing, but a picture of handwritten words had somehow been etched into my thoughts, landing in my heart. If I thought about the upcoming trip home to pack up my grandparents' belongings, I'd see this blurred image of handwriting in my mind.

Even though I got the beautiful opportunity to journey with my Pop the last several weeks of his life, we lacked an exchange of words. Maybe the words I wanted to find now were actually lost words, buried in the deaths of my grandparents.

If only in my mind, I desperately wanted to read these words that were now becoming a legacy of sorts to me.

I became excited at the idea of a treasure hunt in my grandparents' attic. I didn't know what exactly I was looking for, but I knew I'd recognize it when I saw it.

Uncle Hank, my cousin Michael, and myself tackled the daunting task of clearing the attic. One of the first boxes we opened held Grandma's Bible. As I quickly looked through it, so excited and convinced I'd see handwritten words, my uncle said, "She wasn't one to journal, and she wasn't one to talk a lot about it, but she read the Bible every morning." This touched my heart, and I instantly felt connected to

Grandma since this was my heart's passion, feeding on God's Word daily.

As the day progressed with boxes opened and emptied, the dust as unsettling as my searching heart, I didn't find the words.

In the late afternoon of day two of my treasure-hunting-searching-for-the-words-in-my-mind's-eye attic experience, we came upon a stack of letters from Pop's best friend and my heart leaped. I peeked inside a couple of envelopes and saw words from a typewriter. Something told me this was a cool story and maybe the lost handwritten words were enclosed in one of the letters, but there were too many to look through right then, so I put them aside and kept working on emptying the overwhelming number of boxes that my grandparents had accumulated and stored for decades.

For a few days, we continued opening boxes, relishing the memories conjured up by the important treasures of photographs, books, and even the military decorations that deserved a better home than the dusty attic. Even the simple things like trinkets, dishes, clothes, and many boxes of "just junk" brought us into bouts of laughter and good memories. As we matched up the treasures to the family members not able to be there, we united even closer, satisfied that each person would stay connected with perfect gifts found in the attic.

With each box that didn't hold the treasure I was searching for, I let go a tiny bit more. I began to think there were no special handwritten words to be found.

As the doubt grew, so did my regret. I regretted being so far away from my grandparents while they were alive, and I especially regretted not being bigger and stronger than the circumstances that kept me from them. I was realizing too late how much I had wanted them to speak into my life. And now here I was, searching for a legacy of words that only existed in my mind.

I accepted that there were no words to be found after all, and I began carrying the boxes of trash downstairs, concluding my treasure hunt.

And then, just like that, I was holding the handwritten words in my hand, recognizing them instantly, just as I knew I would. Uncle Hank had found them in the last box of file folders.

A box that looked like trash held the treasure. He had decided to go through all the folders of miscellaneous paperwork, "just in case."

Knowing of my search, he called me into the attic and said, "Here it is. This is definitely for you."

I sat down on a nearby box and felt a moment of awe and wonder as I saw the same handwriting etched in my mind for over a month now. It almost didn't even matter what it said because I felt so heard and acknowledged.

But these particular words *did* matter.

On the back of a dry cleaning laundry list order sheet was a list of someone's life goals. I chuckled at the first one, knowing instantly who the author was: Pop.

1. To be able to look forward with enthusiasm and backward with satisfaction
2. To channel my thoughts and action and those around me to produce admiration
3. To search for truth
4. To satisfy statistics
5. To be successful
6. To live a peaceful and contented life up to a ripe old age
7. To outdo my parents

8. To provide my family with all their needs and wants and ensure that they will be respected in society
9. To help the underprivileged
10. To maintain interest
11. To lead a worthwhile life that will give justice to God, myself, and my neighbor
12. To be ready for God's world when this world is finished

He had written the words and they, he and Grandma, had walked them out together. These words gave me, and now others, a legacy to be remembered, reclaimed, and renewed.

If adhered to, it was a laundry list that could help others accomplish what my grandparents had accomplished as they lived a long, happy marriage together. They so beautifully displayed this list with subtle integrity and faith. Throughout their lives, their actions simply and powerfully matched these words.

With the laundry list in hand, I had found what I was looking for—now for the hard work of getting rid of all the trash. We managed to sort through everything in the attic. Sorting through fifty-plus years of storage was no small feat! Most of the trash went out the attic window and into a Dumpster. The personal paperwork, including medical and bank records, needed to be shredded or burned. We chose to burn the old records, and I volunteered for the task since Uncle Hank and Michael were doing all the physical work.

There was a fire pit at the lake resort where we were staying. Off I went with multiple boxes and a lighter. I thought I could dump a box of papers in the pit and light it all on fire. It didn't work that way. They burned very slowly, and I was there for hours. At first, I was pissed off at myself for not knowing to put lighter fluid on the paperwork. It was too late to go to a store, as everything was closed. A strange thing happened, though.

This tedious chore became therapeutic. There was something extremely healing as I watched my grandparents' records burn. It didn't start out feeling like healing. It hurt deeply to see their names burn away. Names are so important, aren't they?

Several years ago, my heart leaped as I overheard one particular name: Opal Broderick. My sister was talking to my mom about Grandma's housecleaner. *Was she related? If so, did they know it?*

I pulled my sister aside and asked her if Opal, the housecleaner, was related to Graham, and she said, "Well, I think she's his grandma." My heart hurt so much because to me her mere presence in their home backed up the "not guilty" verdict her grandson had received so many years ago. *Grandma and Pop wouldn't do that to me. They believed me, didn't they?*

Back then, I told Anne she was mistaken, and I never asked another question about any of it. Fear kept the biggest question unanswered.

The grief was deep, and I almost didn't allow the process. I wanted to run from the fire and tell my uncle I needed to wait until tomorrow to get lighter fluid and finish the task, but I didn't want to let him down. He had taken over my grandfather's bank account, and they shared the same name. Anyone who got hold of these partially burned records could essentially damage his identity.

The desire to help my uncle kept me seated at the fire pit's edge. In my need to push down the grief, I just stared at the dwindling fire. I disappeared into the small flickering flame, realizing that I never really knew if my grandparents believed me or not. I knew that they loved me and it didn't matter to them. *But did they believe me? They* are so close to me. I hate it.

*I'll never know what they thought or believed.* I realized it needed to not matter anymore. I needed to let that need to be believed go up in smoke, just like these old records.

Taking the lighter, I started another fire, and this time it took. I had a fire! Once again, I began throwing medical records into the fire. I stared into the growing flames and watched as the word *record* burned away. Even in their deaths, *especially* in their deaths, I needed to forgive them as if they didn't believe me and love them as if they did believe me. I needed to allow it *all* to burn away. I needed to let go of all the questions and all the lessons I wanted to learn from them and didn't get to. As I watched the smoke billow into the air, I let it all go and freedom engulfed me. Something heavy lifted off me.

Within seconds, my decision was challenged.

What I grabbed next was a stack of checks. As I threw a handful of cleared checks into the fire, I saw her name: *Opal Broderick*. I grabbed the check from the fire and read it in full. The memo said, "Housecleaning," and my heart broke in pieces.

I looked up to the sky, to my God, and moaned. In that moment, I knew I had a choice. I could take back my newly discovered freedom or I could let it continue to burn. With tears streaming down my face, I threw the check back in the fire and watched it slowly turn to ash.

### San Diego, California, April 2015

Once again, I returned home to California only to face another relapse from Matt and another wave of exhaustion, rendering me powerless to make the decisions I knew I needed to make but just couldn't seem to be able to do.

My heart had taken too many relapses, too many betrayals, and too many empty promises. *Or did God simply want me next to Him?*

The anger toward Matt's addiction burned within me one morning as we argued over my lack of trusting him. I was constantly suspicious of him and as we were yelling at each other, I noticed Pop and Hayden's letters sitting on the bookshelf where they had been untouched for weeks.

If history were to repeat itself, the letters would be sitting on a shelf for months and then probably get lost. Disgusted with this, I grabbed the bin holding the letters off the shelf and sat on the step outside, shutting the door to the battleground going on in my home.

It made sense to order the envelopes by date. I couldn't wait to see my pop through someone else's eyes.

It only took about fifteen minutes to get the envelopes in chronological order. A couple of my late Uncle Logan's letters were in the pile. *Why were they in this pile?* Assuming they were misplaced, I set them aside. I was anxious to begin reading, and as I did, the fatigue I felt was quickly being replaced with excitement as I engrossed myself in the project.

The first letter was dated January 27, 1970. The last of the letters was dated January 6, 1987. I had years of reading ahead of me.

*Hi, Virginia and Hank,*

*Just got back from a fast trip up to see my mother. Last time I saw her we sat out on the lawn in the sun, so you can see it's been quite awhile. She looked fine for eighty-eight years. Before I left home, I put a shovel, a jug of water, and chains in the trunk, making sure the jack was also there. For a change, the car ran fine, although I had alerted Don and Janet in case I got stuck. Matter of fact, it ran so good I was trying to figure when I could drive it to Berdan Place. I had tried to strike up a conversation with Flo, but she was noncommittal, being busy with her chewing gum. She is an expert at snapping it. Sounds like someone cracking a whip over a twenty-mule team. She was popping it three cracks every four minutes when I almost hit a dump truck that had no brakelights. After she got her elbow out of the glove compartment and the Christmas packages off the floor, she went back to a conservative two "pops" every ten minutes. We were home around 4:30, and I found your letter in the mailbox. I had to smile at your question: "Would you be interested in coming down for a weekend?" You know ...*

And the letters continued, laced with humor that only the two of them would probably get, but it felt good to be focusing on something that had nothing to do with me or my pain. Or Matt ... or his pain. It was a pleasant distraction, and I enjoyed the pleasantries of Hayden.

After a couple more letters with similar content, I wondered what the other letters were about, the ones from Uncle Logan. *Would it be wrong to read them?* Both he and Pop were no longer living so, I decided it was okay.

There were two letters. One *from* Uncle Logan and one *to* Uncle Logan.

*March 8, 1979*

*Dear son,*

*I need to straighten a few things out with you. I could say you only get out of something what you put into it. I would also say no one really gets something for nothing that really lives to enjoy it.*

*After a person breaks a promise to me, it takes some time for that person to prove himself to me. I still believe this. If you think you have seen your mistakes and intend to change and straighten out your wrongdoing, I commend you with all my heart. I hope you carry through with it.*

*I have always said and believed what I do today: I can lie down when night comes and not regret it. I'm all right. If I can't do this, then I must correct what I think I did wrong.*

*I recall a chaplain asking a definition of ambition. A Filipino sergeant replied, "Look forward with enthusiasm and backward with pleasure." If you can do this, each day has been and will be of great satisfaction for you.*

*There are so many times I can recall of the good times I've had with you and the little things you said and did, which if I had to make a list, it would go beyond ... I can say that so many good times and things you and I did will outnumber and outweigh the wrong or bad times we endured.*

*So let all our unpleasant things be so small that you can only think of the good things.*

*Good night.*

*Love,*

*Daddy*

*       *       *

*February 15, 1981*

*Dear Daddy,*

*Received your letter this morning. Tell me what is happening with Abigail. Why is the whole town talking about her?*

*I talked to Michael yesterday … He is doing good with his job.*

In shock, I scanned the rest of the ancient letter, but I realized there was not another word about me. Frantically I started searching through the other letters. Maybe one got misfiled. There had to be answers here! What did Pop say in reply? Maybe his unmailed letter was in here, just like the one I had found earlier. I mean, it was possible, wasn't it? There *they* were again—invading my space, my heart, my head, and my peace.

The mold on the letter from all the years of these words sitting in an attic box infiltrated my senses. Mold, much like shame, grows over the years and is capable of causing a silent sickness.

It'd be so easy to just lock it all away again. *I mean, why have I gone through all this? Why, oh why, did I ask any questions at all? Why did I go back and into any of this? What is the purpose, if every time there is an answer, a bigger question presents itself?*

All the healing that had taken place over the years of my returning to Little Mountain *almost* came undone, because once again, I felt the darkness of that familiar hallway from so many years ago.

Closing my eyes, I envisioned myself standing in front of the locked bathroom door where I had last seen Abbey. I could hear something … *Was someone singing?*

*Jesus loves me. This I know, for the Bible tells me so. Little ones to Him belong; they are weak but He is strong. Yes, Jesus loves me. Yes, Jesus loves me …*

There was no forceful turning of the knob; there was no kicking of the door.

It was simple; I knocked.

*Click.*

A man opened the door slightly, and Abbey meekly peeked out from behind Him. It was as if they had been waiting patiently for me to figure out the simple solution that was probably so obvious to them. Our eyes met as I accepted the object that He was handing me, a circle. The familiar warmth of forgiveness engulfed me, and I knew it was what I had been searching for all along.

Picking up the letter again, I reread my uncle's question through the eyes of one with a new perspective, one of forgiveness and love, both given and received.

"Why is the whole town talking about her?" I whispered, repeating the words my uncle had written years ago. The hinges squeaked from a door that had been kept shut for far too long and the door opened all the way. Bravely, Abbey stepped out, into freedom.

She stood next to me, grabbed my hand, and said, "They just don't know the truth—that's all. Come on. Let's go." And with that, we walked down the hallway and into our newfound light.

## Epilogue

# *Reunited*

Little Mountain, Kentucky, September 2015

There was no mistaking where the party was. "Welcome to LMS 30-Year High School Renunion! Go Big Blue!"

*Will they remember me? If they do, will they accept me again? Will I remember them? And if I do, can I accept them back in? Has it been too long to feel a connection with anyone here? Where do I say I've been all these years? I didn't share homecoming dance, prom, or graduation here … Will they see the stains of my past?*

"Abigail, it's really you!"

"Come here, girl. Give me a hug!"

"I'm so glad you are here."

"You really drove all the way from California to see us?"

"Do you remember when …?"

And the evening flowed smoothly from there. We talked and laughed and remembered. We reminisced about what it was like to be young and live in Little Mountain. We discussed small-town life and all that we shared together. Blurred memories came into focus.

When conversation shifted to the years I was gone, the

group included me by saying, "You would have loved it, Abigail." I also heard, "I bet you would have gotten Most Likely to Succeed."

When the time came to take the group photo, I volunteered to take the photograph. I mean, it only made sense! I'd be the one capturing the image of the ones who had stayed all through high school, unlike me. That'd be my way of appropriately being a part of it all. Walking to my table, grabbing my camera, John, the former class president, said, "Put that thing down. You can't be in the picture and take it at the same time!"

"Oh, I'll take it. I don't need to be in the picture, John. Really, you guys are all too kind. I am okay not being in it, I'm just happy to be included at all!" I replied, my smile beaming with confidence.

"We will have none of that, girl." He reached out to take my camera. I handed it over, and he quickly gave it to his wife, making it clear that she was the photographer and I was not just an outside observer but also a part of the memory!

I was a part of *them*.

There was an instant, right before he took me by the elbow and guided me to the group waiting on the bleachers, ready for the photo, that I looked into the familiar eyes of kids I had thought were long gone. I realized in that moment that the one recognizing these kids was no longer "long gone" either. She knew these friends, and these friends knew her. These people are part of my heart's home. They knew me and unknowingly sent me out many years ago. I have missed this connection, and I am so grateful to God that He brought me to this thirty-year reunion—not just to celebrate a high school graduation but also to journey home to celebrate something much deeper than a diploma. Innocence reclaimed.

## The Key

There are many doors in the hallway of our lives. Some doors get opened, while others remain closed. For me, the key to knowing which ones to approach is in knowing and obeying the voice of God and having the assurance that He is in complete control, walking it out with me.

That is His joy within me.

The privilege of taking this beautiful journey of walking back into my past was, and still is, beyond my comprehension. There were huge pieces of my life taken away through this crisis, and much was restored in ways I never could have imagined. Nor will I ever be able to find the appropriate words to describe its beauty. The most powerful restoration was that of my identity. The second was that of my voice.

I could never give due justice to my restoration journey, because it's beyond me. But I did try by sharing my experience to the best of my ability. There was so much more that happened that didn't make it in this book. I suppose those moments are between God and I … intimate and sacred.

There were other moments that happened so quickly and I'm left to process them over time from deep within. Like being in church at Communion time, only to be faced with Calvin Cartway as the one to hand me the tray.

Communion is a time of self-examination. *How and what am I keeping from God? Do I need to forgive anyone? Has anyone offended me … and what part of this offense is my responsibly? Have I misperceived anything regarding this issue? And what, Lord, do I need to surrender to you and let go of?* These are the questions I tend to ask myself during this intimate time of worship and confirmation of my faith. It's a sort of "self-check" with whether or not I am honoring God. It's a preparation to receive Him in that moment.

Receiving that tray from Mr. Cartway and making a decision in a moment to choose faith over resentment was empowering.

Regarding the answers that I did not receive, I would have loved to have had a snow globe, or a circle of some sort, readily available to hand to each person who left me with more questions, for I now realize that they weren't put in my path to answer any questions at all. I was to begin the process of true forgiveness, something foreign to the victim in me who wanted justice. I mean, I was entitled to answers, wasn't I? It's part of my victim's rights, isn't it? Yet that is what I had to lay down: my rights.

For years, I proclaimed and even thought I was a forgiving person. But I had not yet counted the cost of what I was forgiving. Flippant forgiveness minus the mourning of what was lost resulted in empty words of "I have forgiven," words that, as a Christian, I knew I was supposed to say. But the reality was that I didn't even know where to begin to truly forgive. Over the years, asking *why* imprisoned me in unforgiveness and established such a root of bitterness that I couldn't embrace freedom.

For me, I suppose the beginning of forgiveness was the resigning of my rights.

The boys in this story were not rapists. I can't call them that because the court said they were not guilty of such a crime. What did that make me, then? I didn't know what to do with that. For years, I waited for someone to give me the key to an unlocked prison. Turns out I held the key and perseverance turned it.

That, to me, is His joy within me.

It was when I knocked and said, "God I'm here. I'm not

going without You this time." He walked me into and out of my past. The key to this has been obedience.

In the midst of experiencing this story you have now read, I'd randomly get phone calls from a man who was a well known television evangelist who called himself a prophet. How he got my phone number, I do not know!

I never answered because I knew it was a gimmick for money, and he would leave recordings of his prophecies on my voice mail. His insights about my life were eerily on target, which freaked me out! I began wondering if perhaps he was a true prophet because he was so accurate about my situation, each and every time.

One day the prophet called while I was dealing with a crisis. I was driving our work van to a safe place so that Matt could not drive it. I was hiding it from him, and I was upset that I had to do such a thing. Desperation got the best of me, and I didn't let the call go to voice mail. This time I picked up the phone.

It was an automated recording, and as I listened, he kept talking about a key. He said that the *right* doors would open and/or close with the *right* key. He said he had a key for me and if I'd just give a donation of such and such amount, I could own this key and the doors that needed to open would be.

In my discouraged state, I considered it. I pushed the pound button to be transferred to an attendant so that I could purchase this anointed key. As I was on hold, I questioned what I was doing and prayed out loud in the safety of my car. I prayed that God would protect me in my vulnerability and if I shouldn't be talking to this guy, to let me know.

At just that moment, the phone disconnected, and I chuckled. However, I wondered about that key. *Is there such a thing, Lord? If so, show me, please.*

The next morning, as I do every morning, I got up and read my Bible. I opened it and landed on Isaiah 33:6:

> *He will be the sure foundation for your times,*
> *a rich store of salvation and wisdom and*
> *knowledge; the fear of the Lord is the key to*
> *this treasure.*

It's the fear of the Lord, what I call obedience to His ways, that is the key. I believe that each trip back to Little Mountain was a turning of the key, unlocking a measure of freedom.

It's not a jury's opinion of me, or my grandparent's belief in me. It's not up to the choices that my husband makes. Those people, those things, while *they* are important to me, they are not the sure foundation of my life.

Partway through my journey, when the confusing and elusive (albeit concise) thought came that one day on the beach, when I was told *Your justice is My joy within you*, I continued searching because, honestly, that answer wasn't good enough for me. I had not realized yet that joy is not just an emotion. It can be a deliberate choice. I wanted a real and clear absolute "thing" to solve my problem. That's what was so attractive about the simplicity of a real key! I wanted to stick a key in a lock, turn it, and walk through a door, out of the hallways of confusion. I wanted the injustices to be reversed because that is what I thought was owed to me.

But God kept sending me back into a place of question that didn't appear to be giving me any answers. The obedience it took to keep returning amidst the injustices going on in my marriage did not come from my own strength.

All those years ago, I left town right after the court case, allowing twelve jurors *and* the court of public opinion to define me. The experience also shut the door to a big part of my true self: love.

Sometimes I wonder about that day in front of the court clerk and what would have happened had I simply turned and starting singing with that little boy. Jesus loving me was the solution the whole time; I was just stuck behind walls of shame and couldn't sing it, not yet anyway.

Maybe, God needed me to go *reclaim* that abandoned part and love her/me back to wholeness. It took obedience to do this because in dissociating myself at such a young age, I wasn't aware that a part of me was even missing.

But God didn't give up. He wanted me whole. He wants Matt whole. He wants *you* whole. He wants us all wholly loved and known. The intimacy with God that I experienced changed the foundation of my soul to the point that I can now look at Matt and see that he has his own Gilgal to journey around and through. I believe he will find it because He knows Him as well as I do. Today, our dynamic has changed. We honor one another's journey today. I have compassion where I once had cold judgment. I have healthy boundaries in place instead of angry walls of isolation. As I watch Matt embrace truth, I believe he will be okay. Addiction has done serious damage to our marriage and I do not know what is next. What I do know is that my heart is completely surrendered and open to whatever direction God will tell me to go.

I believe we will each be okay, not matter what.

In the beginning of all this, before ever getting on that first airplane, I was living outside the circle of my own wounded soul, peering in, wondering why I couldn't even look in the mirror. The most important of my relationships, the one with my children, was wounded, and I had a skewed misperception of our lives.

Throughout this process, in the hallway of it all, I have opened the door of my heart and embraced the healing necessary, allowing our family to focus on forgiveness and healing.

Today I have the inner peace that was taken from me, and I have healthy relationships. Not perfect, but healthy.

After all, even the most beautiful picket fences have flaws in them.